In an era of wars and revolutions

American socialist cartoons of the mid twentieth century

By Carlo and others

Edited by Sean Matgamna

In an era of wars and revolutions
American socialist cartoons of the mid twentieth
century, by Carlo, Laura Gray, Seaman, Robert
Minor, and others

Edited by Sean Matgamna

Printed by Imprint Digital, Exeter EX5 5HY

Published 2013 by Phoenix Press
20E Tower Workshops
Riley Road
London SE1 3DG

This work is licensed under the Creative Commons Attribution 2.5 Generic License. To view a copy of this license, visit
http://creativecommons.org/licenses/by/2.5/ or send a letter to Creative Commons, 444 Castro Street, Suite 900, Mountain View, California, 94041, USA.

I dedicate this book to the memory of all the revolutionary socialists (revolutionary anarchists included) of the dark middle years of the 20th century who kept the Red Flag clean and raised it up as high as they could reach; and to those who continue that work now.

The cartoons are by Carlo (Jesse Cohen), Laura Gray (Slobe), "Seaman", Fred Ellis, Robert Minor, and others. Each is marked with its date (except a few where we have been unable to retrace it). The originals appeared in issues of those dates of the socialist papers *Labor Action, New Militant, Socialist Appeal, The Militant,* the *Daily Worker, The Liberator,* and the *Workers' Monthly*. Previous page: 1 May 1925.

Contents

Introduction 1

Timeline 4

1 Them and us 9
Perceptions of capitalism 10
Rich man, poor man, beggar man, thief 24

2 The class struggle 31
Wages, prices, rents, profit, taxes 32
Labour movements 41
German workers after the defeat of 1923 49
Women workers 51
The economic front 53
The political front 62
The battle of ideas 69

3 Independent working-class politics 85
Plutocrat democracy 85
For a US Labour Party 91

4 Proposals to the working class 99

5 Jim Crow: fighting racism 119

6 Roosevelt and the New Deal 135

7 Stalinism 141
The USSR 143
The Popular Front 148

The Moscow Trials 153
The murder of Leon Trotsky 158
Parrot party: the CP USA 161
The Stalin-Hitler pact 175

8 Fascism 179
Native fascism 180
Hitlerism 184
Catholic reaction 186
Anti-semitism and other bigotries 188

9 World War 193
On the road to war 194
The World War 200
Taking the profit out of war 205
Labour in the war 211

10 Civil liberty 219
The Minneapolis case 227
Sacco and Vanzetti 232

11 The war is over 237
The victors 239
Conquered Germany 248
The hope of humanity: a working-class socialist revolution 252

12 In the shadow of nuclear war 263
The atomic bomb 265
Stalin's empire 274
The witch-hunt republic 278
US imperialism 285
A permanent arms economy 292

13 World War Three? 295
Colonial revolts 296
Korea 303
Toward a Third World War? 306

Introduction

That "one picture can be worth a thousand words" is true, but only up to a point. A photograph or a painting can not properly nail down, explain or explore ideas. A complicated piece of writing has no visual equivalent.

Yet a well-done cartoon is a powerful political weapon. A few bold strokes by an artist can convey an idea more vividly and fix it more firmly in the viewer's mind than would an editorial or an article.

A cartoon is drawn to convey an idea, a point of view, an interpretation of what it depicts, and its meaning. Cartoons by their nature simplify, caricature, exaggerate, lampoon, and play with archetypal images.

A cartoon is highly subjective, yet it draws on commonly recognised symbols. The image, idea, interpretation fuse in the drawing. Drawn to convey an idea of people, things, institutions, classes, states, and of their inter-relationships, a cartoon distills the artist's conception of what is essential in those people, events, entities, institutions, relationships.

The cartoonist is licensed to distort everyday reality so as to bring out a view, a 'seeing', analysis, critique, historical perspective of it. Its ciphers, emblems, archetypes vary to allow for the artist's individual slant (like, in this collection, Carlo's characteristic rendition of the top hat-fat archetypical bourgeois laughing at the gullibility or helplessness of workers).

All of a cartoon, all its details and references, are consciously or subconsciously chosen to convey a point of view, a nailed-down perception, a historical perspective. In old socialist cartoons the worker is always bigger and stronger than his enemies. He needs only to be awakened to an awareness of his strength.

It is almost always a "he". The socialists who drew these cartoons were, themselves and their organisations, militant for women's rights, but little of that is in their work.

One of the difficulties with old socialist cartoons for a modern viewer is that the stereotype-capitalist wears a top hat and is stout or very fat. In some early 20th century British labour movement cartoons he is named, simply, "Fat". Fat now, in our health-conscious days, is seen as a characteristic of lumpenised workers and other "lower orders" people.

Much contemporary comedy is a hate-ridden depiction of the poor, the disadvantaged, the excluded, the badly educated, by physical type – fat and slobby. Where most of the old racial and national caricatures have been shamed and chased into the underbrush, no longer tolerable to decent people of average good will, the old social-Darwinian racism against the poor is rampant still, unashamed and not often denounced.

Even so, the old symbols, the fat capitalist and the big powerful worker, are still intelligible. They depict truths of our times as well as of their own. These cartoons still live.

They portray US politics, governments, the class struggle, the labour movement, America's "Jim Crow" racism, Stalinism at its zenith, Roosevelt's New Deal, Harry Truman's "Fair Deal", Senator Joe McCarthy, McCarthyism. They present clean and stark class-struggle socialist politics, counterposed to both capitalism and Stalinism.

A few are from the 1920s, but mainly they cover the quarter century after the victory of Hitler in Germany in 1933. and the definitive consolidation of Stalinism in the USSR.

Across the decades, they still carry the emotional hostility to the master class and solidarity with their victims that they were drawn to convey; the socialists' abhorrence of the Stalinist atrocities that discredited and disgraced the name of socialism (they themselves were often among the targets); the desire, hope and drive for a re-made world — a socialist world. They blaze with anger and hatred against the horrors of America's all-contaminating Jim Crow racism.

These cartoons were of their time, and what their time and earlier times led socialists to expect of the future. They were often mistaken. Government repression during World War Two was less fierce than the severe persecution of socialists and militant trade unionists in World War One and afterwards, led them to expect.

In the later 1940s, like most observers, they saw World War Three looming. In fact, the world settled into a prolonged "balance of terror" after Russia developed an atom bomb in 1949 and the USA and Russia fought a proxy war on Korean soil which ended in stalemate. The economic collapse which the experience of the 1930s led them to expect did not come (though in fact the long capitalist upswing took off only with the Korean war boom of 1950-3). Plutocratic democracy in the USA, during the war and after it, proved far less frail than the Marxists feared it would.

Over many years I have collected photocopies of these cartoons, buried as they were in files of old publications for six, seven or eight decades. I think others will be moved by them too.

What Peadar Kearney wrote fifty years after their time of the Fenians, the left-wing Irish Republicans of the 1860s and 70s, speaks to the socialists of the era covered by this book as well.

"Some fell by the wayside
Some died 'mid the stranger,
And wise men have told us
That their cause was a failure;
But they stood by old Ireland
And never feared danger.
Glory O, glory O,
To the bold Fenian men!"

Sean Matgamna, December 2013

Timeline

1929: *October:* Wall Street financial crash. By 1930-1 this feeds through to a world economic depression which lasts, with only minor upticks, through to World War 2 in 1939.

1933: *January:* Hitler becomes Chancellor of Germany. *February:* on pretext of Reichstag fire, constitutional freedoms suspended, thousands of Communists and Social-Democrats arrested. *March:* after new elections, with CP and SPD banned from campaigning, parliament votes dictatorial powers to Hitler. *May:* despite offers by Social-Democrat trade unions to cooperate, Hitler takes over the unions, turns them into a state "Labour Front", and sends union leaders to concentration camps. Also 1933, *March:* Franklin D Roosevelt takes office in USA and begins New Deal programme of reformist state-spending measures to mitigate Great Depression.

1934: *May-August:* Big Teamsters' (truck-drivers') strike in Minneapolis, led by Trotskyists.

1934-8: Great Terror in the USSR. All known Trotskyists, and most surviving Bolsheviks, are wiped out by Stalinist repression.

1935: *May:* USSR signs "Laval-Stalin" pact with France: Stalin declares that he "understands and fully approves" France's military policy. *August:* At its "Seventh Congress", the Stalin-controlled Communist International codifies the Popular Front policy (internationally, pursuit of alliances for the USSR with France and Britain, against Germany; in each country, class-collaboration with bourgeois forces judged democratic or liberal or even just anti-German). *September:* Nuremberg laws deprive Jews of civil rights in Germany. *November:* CIO breaks away from old craft-unionist AFL to form a new industrial-unionist centre in USA.

1936: *March:* Hitler occupies the Rhineland zone demilitarised under the Treaty of Versailles after World War One. *June:* General strike in France. *July:* Civil war breaks out in Spain, as workers and peasants resist a fascist military coup against the recently-elected republican government. *August:* First Moscow show trial, in which Stalin gets old Bolsheviks, Lenin's closest collaborators, condemned to death on trumped-up charges. Other show trials follow in January 1937 and March 1938. *December* (to February 1937): Big sit-down strike against General Motors, high point of a wave of battles which builds mass industrial unions in basic industry for the first time in USA.

1937: *May:* Stalinists and their allies start open military repression of revolutionary socialists and anarchists in republican Spain.

1938: *March:* Hitler annexes Austria. *September:* a congress of Trotskyists proclaims the Fourth socialist and communist International. *September:* Hitler grabs the Sudeten areas of Czechoslovakia. *October:* Munich agreement: France and Britain ratify Hitler's annexation. *November:* "Kristallnacht", organised pogroms against Jews throughout Germany.

1939: *March:* Hitler seizes rest of Czechoslovakia. *April:* Spanish civil war ends with victory for fascists. *August:* Hitler-Stalin pact. *September:* Germany (1 Sep) and USSR (17 Sep) invade Poland. World war breaks out. *November:* Stalin invades Finland.

1940: *April:* Germany invades Norway, and follows up by conquering most of Western Europe within a couple of months (blitzkrieg). Also *April:* The US Trotskyist movement, which as the Nazis sweep across Europe soon will become almost the only sizeable Trotskyist movement in the world able to operate openly, splits after dispute over attitudes to the USSR invasions of Finland and Poland. James P Cannon leads one faction, Max Shachtman another. Trotsky backs Cannon. *August:* Trotsky murdered by Stalinist agent.

1941: *June:* Hitler invades USSR. USSR joins World War 2 as ally of UK. *July:* USA imposes economic embargo on Japan. *September:* USSR and Britain invade and take control of Iran. *December:* Japan attacks US base at Pearl Harbour, in the Pacific. US joins World War 2. *August:* US sets up Office of Price Administration (OPA), with powers to control rents and retail prices (to 1947).

1942: *January:* Wannsee conference fixes detailed plans for mass slaughter of Jews. Nazis kill up to six million over the next few years.

1943: *February:* USSR forces push back Nazis at Stalingrad, turning the tide of the war in the East. Over the next two years, USSR forces advance into eastern and central Europe.

1944: *January:* Communist Party of USA dissolves itself into a "Communist Political Association". *July:* Bretton Woods conference (dominated by Keynes from UK and Harry Dexter White from US) maps post-war arrangements for capitalist world trade and finance. *December:* massacre of Trotskyists by Stalinists in Greece.

1945: *February:* Yalta conference between US, UK, and USSR to discuss post-war carve-ups (followed by Potsdam conference in July-August). *April-May:* Russian troops take Berlin. End of war in Europe. Socialists, and not only socialists, expect mass unemployment and economic disruption to follows, as after World War 1. In fact, US unemployment rises more mildly, to 7.3% in 1949, and then declines. Economic output per head in France in 1945 is only half the 1939 level, but it recovers to the 1939 level by 1949 and then grows fairly fast in the Korean war boom (1950-3), which turns out to be the start of two decades of strong economic expansion in the advanced capitalist countries.

1945: *April:* Roosevelt dies; is succeeded by Harry S Truman, who wins 1948 election and is in office until 1953. *June:* Germany put under "Four Power Occupation". USSR controls East Germany and East Berlin; Britain, France, and the USA, collaborating with each other, control West

Germany and West Berlin. *July:* Labour wins big victory in UK general election and goes on to make more reforms and nationalisations than expected. *July:* Communist Party of USA reconstitutes itself. *August:* Indonesian nationalists declare independence. This independence will finally be recognised by the colonial power, the Netherlands, in 1949, after four years of war by the Indonesians against Japanese troops, then British troops, then Dutch troops. *August:* US atom-bombs Hiroshima and Nagasaki, and occupies Japan. *October* (and following months): massacre of Trotskyists by Stalinists in Greece. *November:* United Auto Workers calls big strike against General Motors — start of a strike wave in the USA in 1946-7 which was the biggest ever in the world up to that date.

1946: *March* — to October 1949: civil war in Greece between Stalinist-led forces and right-wing government militarily backed by UK and US. *April:* USSR forces withdraw from Iran (after US diplomatic pressure: British troops had withdrawn by March). *July:* US concedes independence to the Philippines; gives military aid to local government in long war that follows against Stalinist-led Huk guerrillas.

1947: US workers' upsurge ebbs. *June:* US Congress passes anti-union Taft-Hartley Act. It bans wildcat strikes, solidarity or political strikes, secondary boycotts, secondary and mass picketing, and closed shops. *August:* Britain cedes independence to India.

1948: *February:* Stalinists take full control in Czechoslovakia, where until then there was some autonomous political life. *April:* US starts "Marshall Plan" aid to bolster its allies in Europe. *May-June:* Open breach between USSR and Yugoslavia, where Stalinists have won power autonomously. *June* 1948 to May 1949: USSR blockades Berlin. Britain and the USA airlift supplies to West Berlin. *December:* Alger Hiss indicted for perjury. After this, witch-hunting of leftists (called McCarthyism from 1950) escalates in the USA, reaching a peak during the Korean war, and abating gradually in the mid-1950s.

1949: *January:* Maoists capture Beijing; then Shanghai (May); proclaim "People's Republic of China" (October). US-backed forces of Chiang Kai Shek and Guomindang retreat to Taiwan. *May-October:* Germany de facto divided into two states, the "Federal Republic" (West), and the "Democratic Republic" (East). West Berlin becomes an enclave within East Germany, closely linked to but not formally part of the Federal Republic. *August:* USSR explodes its first atom bomb: beginning of the "balance of terror".

1949-53: Tightening of Stalinist control in Eastern Europe. Show trials of Stalinist party leaders deemed unreliable, such as Slansky in Czechoslovakia and Rajk in Hungary.

1950: *June:* Start of Korean war. The war reaches stalemate in mid-51, and then armistice in July 1953.

1953: *March:* Death of Stalin. This is followed, eventually, by a slow and limited "thaw". *July:* Workers' rising against Stalinism in East Germany.

1954: *March-May:* Vietnamese Stalinists defeat French forces at the battle of Dien Bien Phu. A partition of Vietnam follows, with the North under Stalinist rule and the South under US protection. *November:* Start of Algerian war of independence against France, which will end in victory in 1962.

1956: *March*: New USSR leader Nikita Khrushchev's speech from February denouncing Stalin becomes public. *June*: Workers' uprising in Poznan, in Poland. This is bloodily repressed, but by October reform-Stalinists gain control in Poland without USSR invasion. *October-November*: revolutionary workers' uprising against Stalinism in Hungary, eventually crushed by USSR troops. Also *October-November*: Britain, France, and Israel jointly invade Egypt in reprisal for nationalisation of Suez Canal; they withdraw under pressure from USA.

1
Them and us

"The working class and the employing class have nothing in common... Between these two classes a struggle must go on until the workers of the world organise as a class, take possession of the means of production, and abolish the wage system." — Preamble to the constitution of the Industrial Workers of the World, 1905

"Impartiality as between the strong and the weak is the virtue of the slave" — James Connolly

Perceptions of capitalism

23 July 1945

Inseparable

Above: 13 September 1939. Right: early 1920s.

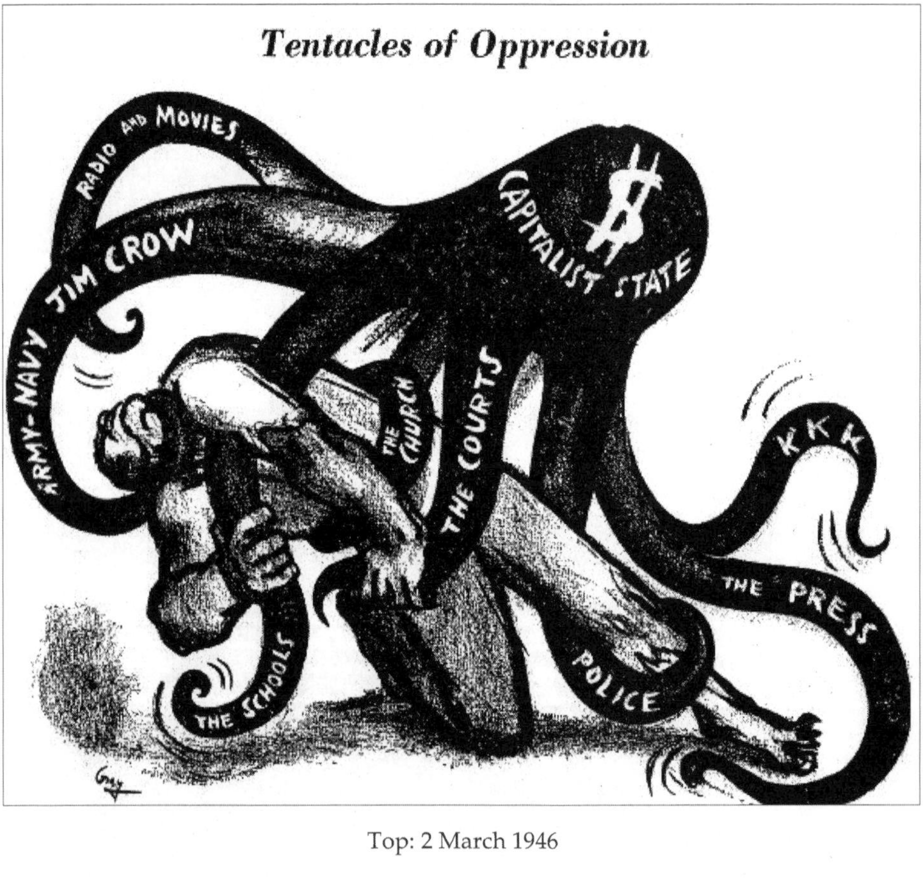

Top: 2 March 1946

Above: 17 October 1939. Below: 27 January 1941.

"STANDARD BUSINESS PRACTICES"

Above: 5 April 1942. Below: 12 April 1942. The small figure is inscribed "Standard Oil", and the flag " I G Farben Uber Alles". In 1941, an investigation exposed close links between the US corporation Standard Oil and I G Farben, which produced Zyklon B used in Holocaust gas chambers. But the investigation was dropped after business pressure.

Above: 9 September 1944. Below: 19 May 1945.

Above: 3 December 1945. Right: 28 April 1925: worker thrown out of a job by capitalist overproduction.

Above: 12 April 1947. Below: 14 July 1947. The words here are typical of 1930s gangster movies; the "see" for emphasis was typical of the actor Edward G Robinson (who in fact visited Leon Trotsky in Mexico at the end of the 1930s).

Top: 27 December 1948. Left: 29 September 1941. The capitalist is one working for the Roosevelt regime for a token wage (he says: "Look at me! I only make a dollar a year"), but the money bags are labelled "government contracts". Right: 6 August 1951.

Above: 2 March 1946. Below: 29 April 1946.

Above: 17 September 1925: "The Checkweighman". Checkweighman was an elected trade-union position in coal mines: he checked weight of coal to stop bosses cheating workers paid by the ton. Below: 27 March 1928

Above: 19 December 1924. Below: 4 July 1925

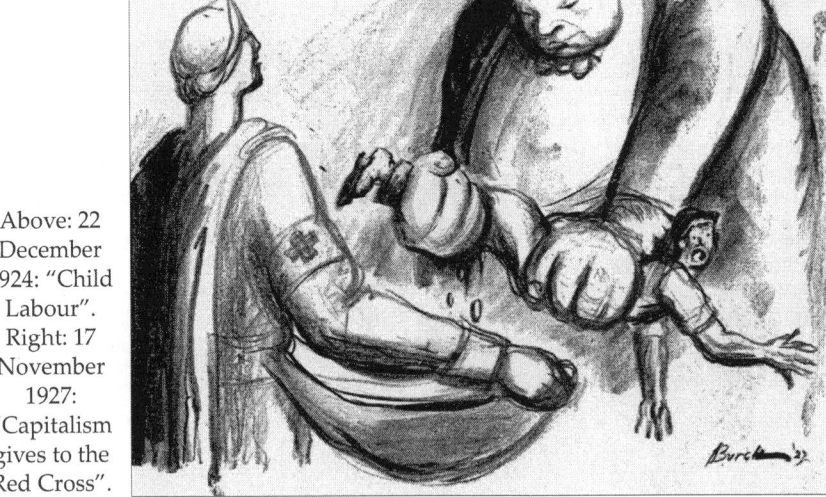

Above: 22 December 1924: "Child Labour". Right: 17 November 1927: "Capitalism gives to the Red Cross".

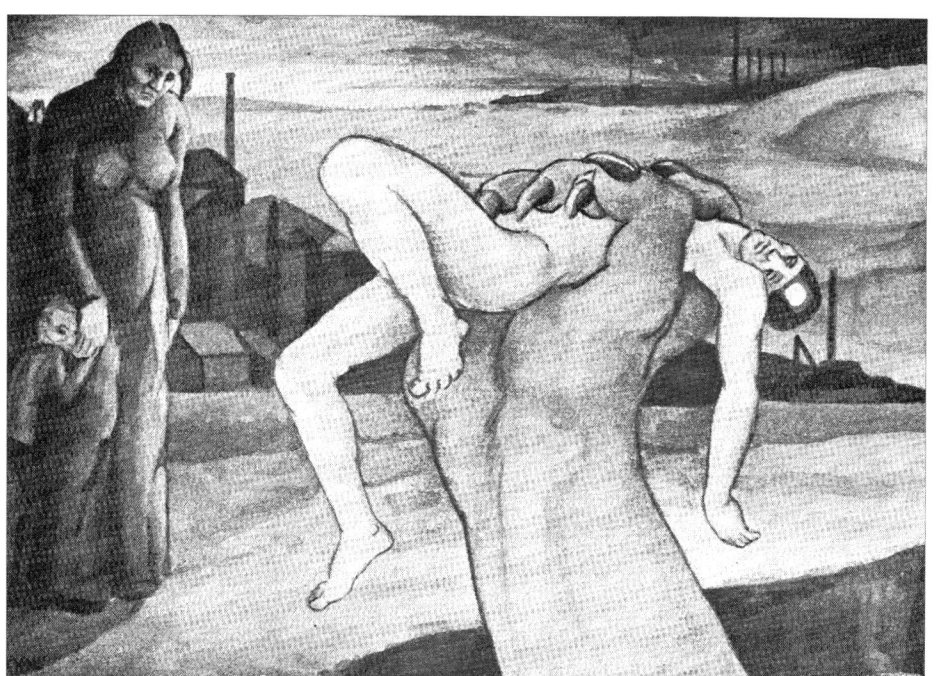

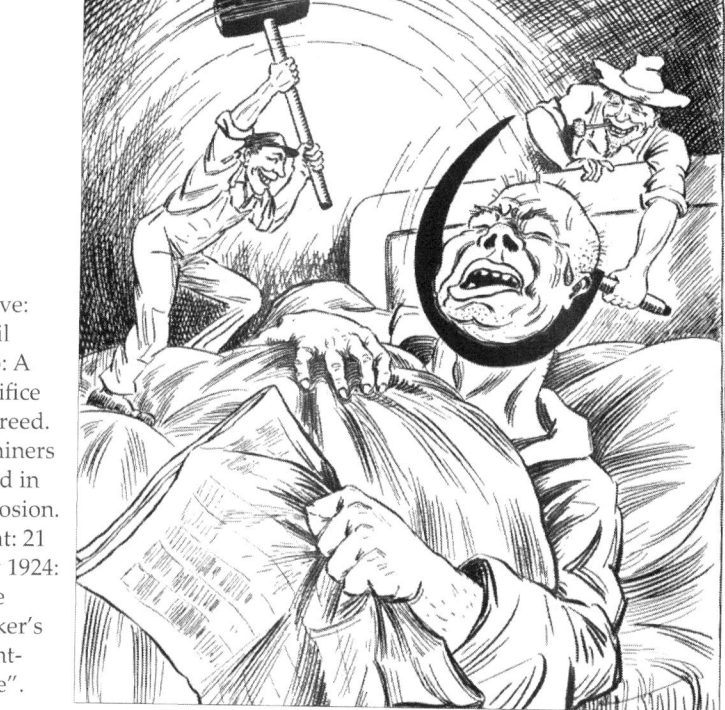

Above: April 1925: A Sacrifice to Greed. 51 miners killed in explosion. Right: 21 May 1924: "The Banker's Nightmare".

Rich man, poor man, beggar man, thief

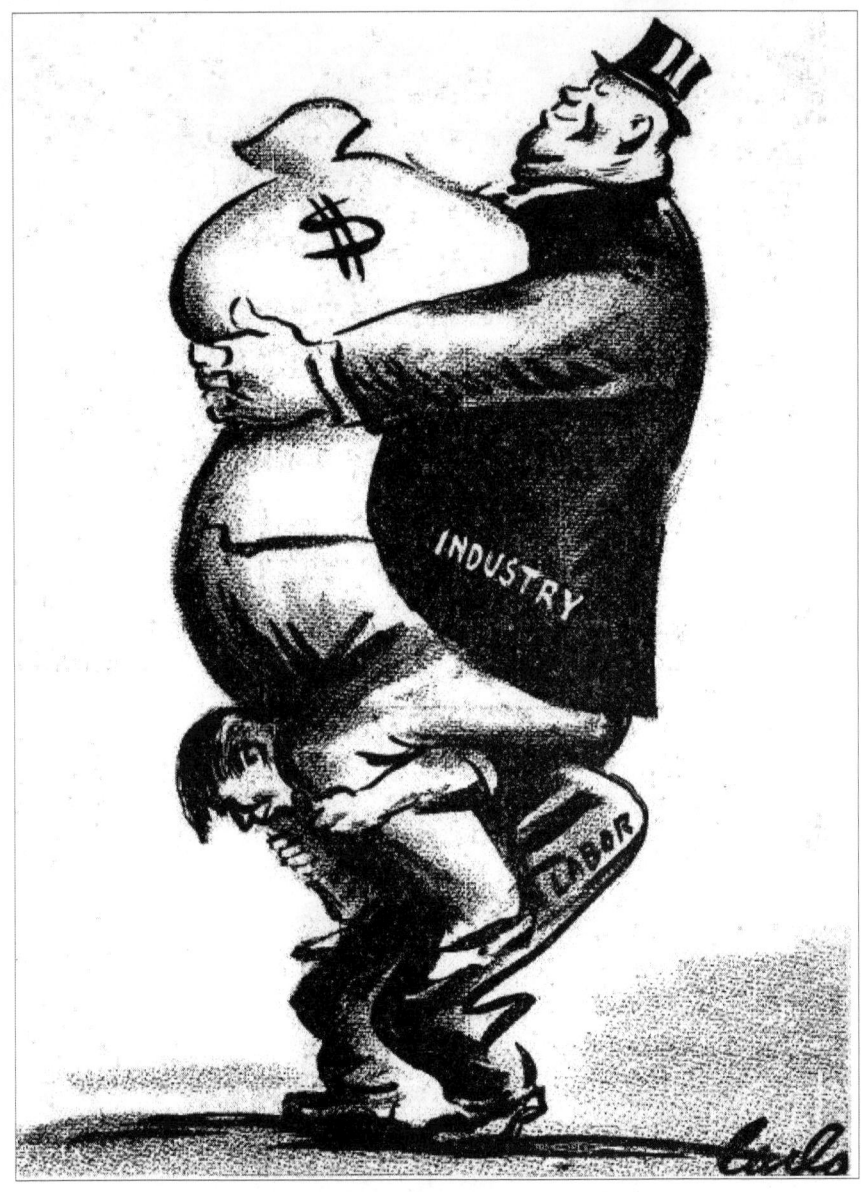

11 May 1942: "Equal Sacrifice"

Above: 22 Dec 1941. Below: 2 Feb 1928. "Team Work".

Above: 21 April 1941. Below: 27 May 1946.

The "dollar-a-year men" were business bosses doing government work for expenses plus $1 a year. They also, of course, got their dividends and valuable access for contracts. Above: 31 August 1942.
Right: 26 January 1942.

14 September 1942. In April 1942 President Roosevelt called for a freeze on wages. Wages were limited to 15% above the levels of 1 January 1941. Despite a theoretical freeze on prices, the cost of living rose much more than 15%.

We Gotta Bear the Burden Equally!

Above: 5 July 1943.
Right (1920s):
"Rationalised".

4 February 1946.

2
The class struggle

"For the first time since a workers' movement has existed, the struggle is being conducted pursuant to its three sides — the theoretical, the political, and the practical-economic (resistance to the capitalists). It is precisely in this, as it were, concentric attack, that the strength and invincibility of the German movement lies" –
Frederick Engels, 1874

Wages, prices, rents, profit, taxes

12 October 1942. Previous page: 1 September 1947. In the USA, wages, prices, and rents were all supposedly frozen during and for a while after the war, but in fact prices rose faster than wages. Consumer price inflation ran especially high in the USA from mid-1946 to the end of 1948, with a peak of 19.7% per year in March 1947.

1 April 1946.

2 November 1942.

Standing In The Way

Just A Leaking Bucket

Above: 13 July 1946. Right: 20 July 1946. The leaking bucket is labelled "New OPA" (the official price-control body).

5 August 1946.

Wages and prices were both supposedly frozen during and for a while after the war, but in fact prices rose faster than wages. Above: 7 October 1946. Right: 21 October 1946.

Wolf At The Door

Above: 28 December 1946, as wartime rent controls were eased. Right: 26 June 1924. "Grab him".

Above: 8 Sep 1947. The donkey and the elephant are symbols of the Democratic Party and Republican Party (GOP) respectively. Below: 6 June 1949.

Above: 25 November 1957.
Right: 25 August 1947.
"Investigating the price conspiracy". The figure with the magnifying glass is inscribed "Attorney General Clark". Prices had risen especially fast in 1946-7.

Labour movements

25 November 1957. After a workers' demonstration on 4 May 1886 in Chicago, eight activists — the "Haymarket Martyrs" — were convicted on trumped-up charges, and four of them hanged.

Above: 27 April 1935.
Right: 21 June 1947

30 December 1946.

Above: 9 March 1946. An appeal for solidarity with the General Motors strike of 1945-6, which was the first big strike since the 1930s and the first battle in the great strike wave of 1946-7. Right: 2 December 1940.

Only Answer To The Labor-Haters

Industrial vs. Craft Unionism

Above: 8 June 1946. Right: 25 October 1941. Teamsters' Local 544 was led by Trotskyists. The CIO, a confederation of industrial-unions, broke away in 1935 from the old craft-unionist American Federation of Labor (AFL) and grew fast in the 1930s. It reunified with the AFL in 1955.

Above: 25 April 1949. The treaty to set up NATO ("war pact") was signed on 4 April 1949. Below: 11 Nov 1946.

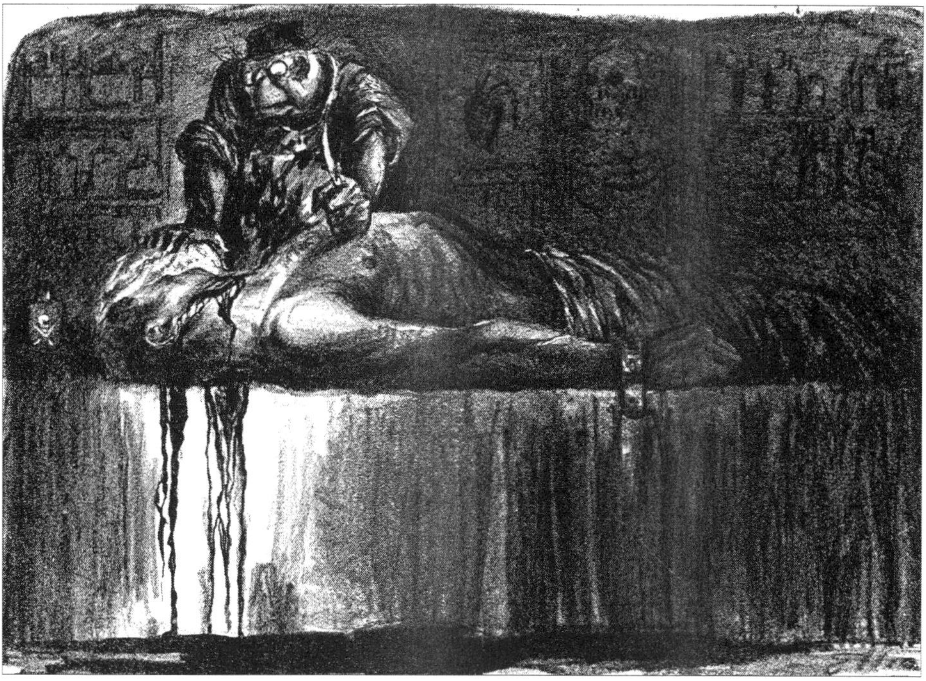

Above: January 1925: "Letting the red out". The surgeon is rightwing US trade union leader Sam Gompers. Below: May 1925: "The Big Fellows". But the Anglo-Russian Trade Union Committee, shaped by Stalinist policy, became not a vehicle for rank and file action, but a cover for British trade union leaders who sold out the General Strike of 1926.

Above: 4 March 1926. The tiny figure is reciting, from Kipling, "The East is the East, and the West is the West, and never the twain shall meet", and being told by an insect: "You're a liar". Below: caricature of the 1925 convention of the American Federation of Labor, with all the delegates prosperous men with cigars, and the ghost of Sam Gompers in the chair.

German workers after the defeat of 1923

In 1923 Germany went through economic collapse and hyperinflation. In October 1923 the Communist Party bungled a revolutionary situation and went down to defeat. Above: February 1924: "Famine and death, the legitimate child of bankrupt capitalism, threatening the working men, women and children of Germany. Will you help?"

January 1924. Starving German children depicted in a Communist International campaign for working-class financial support for German workers.

Women workers

Above: 3 March 1928. Right: 6 March 1926.

The economic front

9 May 1939.

A Lesson in Democracy

Above: 19
April 1947.
Right: 8
May 1950.

Above: 9 May 1939. Below: 26 January 1946. The GM (General Motors) strike of 1945-6 was the first battle in the big 1946-7 strike wave.

31 March 1941. The figure at top right represents President Franklin D Roosevelt. This was before the US entered the war (December 1941).

24 November 1941. In October 1941 workers in the "captive" coal mines, those owned by steel companies and the like to secure their coal supplies, had struck to demand a "union shop", a rule that all workers must be members of a union. "Open shop" is the converse, a workplace where there is no rule for union membership: it implies an anti-union regime. The right-hand figure is President Franklin D Roosevelt.

Shake Them Down

D-Day for Labor

Above: 20 March 1944. Right: 4 June 1945, a year after the military D-Day when US and UK troops landed in France.

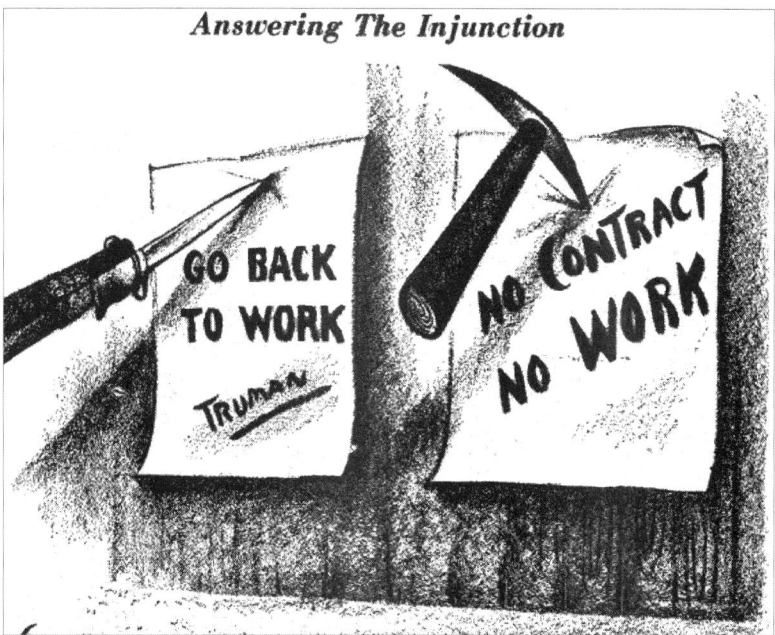

Above: 21 November 1949. Zinc miners in New Mexico began a 15-month strike in early 1950. Below: 30 November 1946. In November-December 1946 US coal miners struck, defying a court injunction.

Above: 23 September 1925: "On Strike. Tie 'Em Up" (about a strike in the ports). Right: 23 December 1940, titled "And we're not waiting for Christmas".

Smash It Open!

Above: 2 February 1946. Right: 16 February 1927. "Ford sits on his rocks". Henry Ford had said: "Business conditions in America are as solid as a rock".

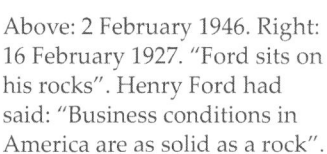

The political front

The Watchdog of Capitalism

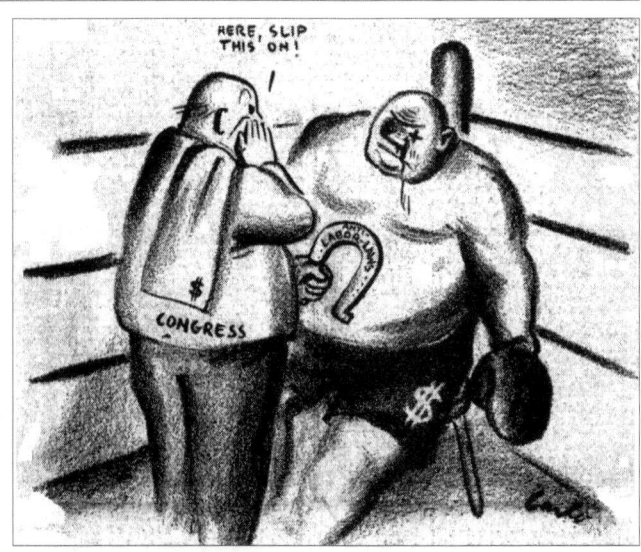

Above: 7 January 1946. Right: 12 May 1947. The horseshoe is inscribed: "Anti-labour laws". The anti-union Taft-Hartley Act became law in June 1947.

Above: 9 March 1942. Right: 13 September 1927: "Protection of the law".

Above: 18 July 1939. Below: 5 July 1948.

16 June 1939, in the run-up to World War Two

10 July 1943

Above: 10 May 1948. Right: 7 July 1947. The winning boxer's two gloves are inscribed "Democrats" and "Republicans". The figures crying "We wuz robbed" are union leaders William Green and Philip Murray, The defeated boxer's gloves are inscribed "Postcard Campaign"

Above: 1 June 1946. Right: 22 Feb 1947. Wall St, in New York, is the centre of big finance capital in the USA.

The battle of ideas

"To say that politically conscious leaders cannot divert the movement from the path determined by the interaction of environment and elements is to ignore the simple truth that the conscious element participates in this interaction and in the determination of the path. Catholic and monarchist labour unions in Europe are also an inevitable result of the interaction of environment and elements, but it was the consciousness of priests and not that of socialists that participated in this interaction" – Lenin, A Talk with Defenders of Economism

"Theory Also Becomes a Force Once It Seizes Hold of the Masses!"

February 1926

Above: 18 May 1927. Below: 2 September 1927

Above: 29 Nov 1954. The National Right to Work Committee was founded in 1954 by a group of ultra-conservative businessmen, and promoted "right-to-work" laws and constitutional amendments in many states. These have nothing to do with guarantees of employment, but instead guarantee bosses the right to hire non-union workers. Below: 19 Jan 1926: "I know what this Bolshevism means, Bill. It means us". Previous page: 5 April 1942.

"Our Interests" Must Be Defended!

What the Last War for "Democracy" Was About!

Above: 7 March 1939. Right: 21 March 1939

Above: 9 Sep 1957. Right: 14 January 1946

Top: 9 February 1935. In January-March 1935 eighteen farm labour organisers, some linked to the Communist Party, faced up to 14 years jail for violation of California's Criminal Syndicalism Act. Hearst was the Murdoch of his day, and the SF Examiner one of his papers. Right: 9 September 1940

1 July 1940.

Above: 19 May 1941.
Right: 16 December 1940.

NEWS ITEM: EUGENE GRACE, HEAD OF BETHLEHEM STEEL, GETS SALARY RAISE FROM $271,000 TO $375,000 A YEAR

(STEEL WORKERS hand offering "$1-A-DAY WAGE INCREASE"; small figure atop a "$" globe shouting "YOU'RE THE ONE THAT'S CAUSING INFLATION!")

20 July 1942

30 September 1946

Above. 23 February 1942.
Right: 1 July 1944

28 June 1943

21 December 1942.

Above: 13 October 1947. The anti-union Taft-Hartley Law was passed in 1947. Right: 17 May 1943

Above: 27 October 1947

3
Independent working-class politics
Plutocrat democracy

"The emancipation of the working classes must be conquered by the working classes themselves" — Rules of the First International

"The first step in the revolution by the working class is to raise the proletariat to the position of ruling class, to win the battle of democracy" — Communist Manifesto.

Above: 5 August 1940. Conscription was introduced in September 1940, over a year before the US entered World War 2.
Right: 27 May 1940

Above: 29 July 1944.
Right: 11 April 1939

The Champions of Democracy at Work!

Above: 21 March 1939. In 1937-8 the US Congress discussed the "Ludlow amendment", calling for a referendum before the US could declare war. The Trotskyists critically backed it. Right: 21 June 1948. After the expiry of the 1940 conscription law, a new law was passed in June 1948, and continued in operation until 1973.

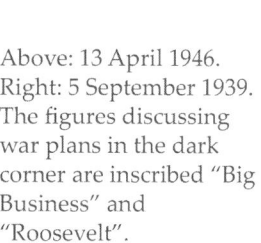

Above: 13 April 1946. Right: 5 September 1939. The figures discussing war plans in the dark corner are inscribed "Big Business" and "Roosevelt".

Above: 30 March 1941. Below: June 1928. "The Slimy Trail"

No Back-Seat Drivers!

Above: 20 January 1941.
Right: 16 November 1946.
The elephant and the donkey are symbols of the US Republican and Democratic Parties.

For a US Labour Party

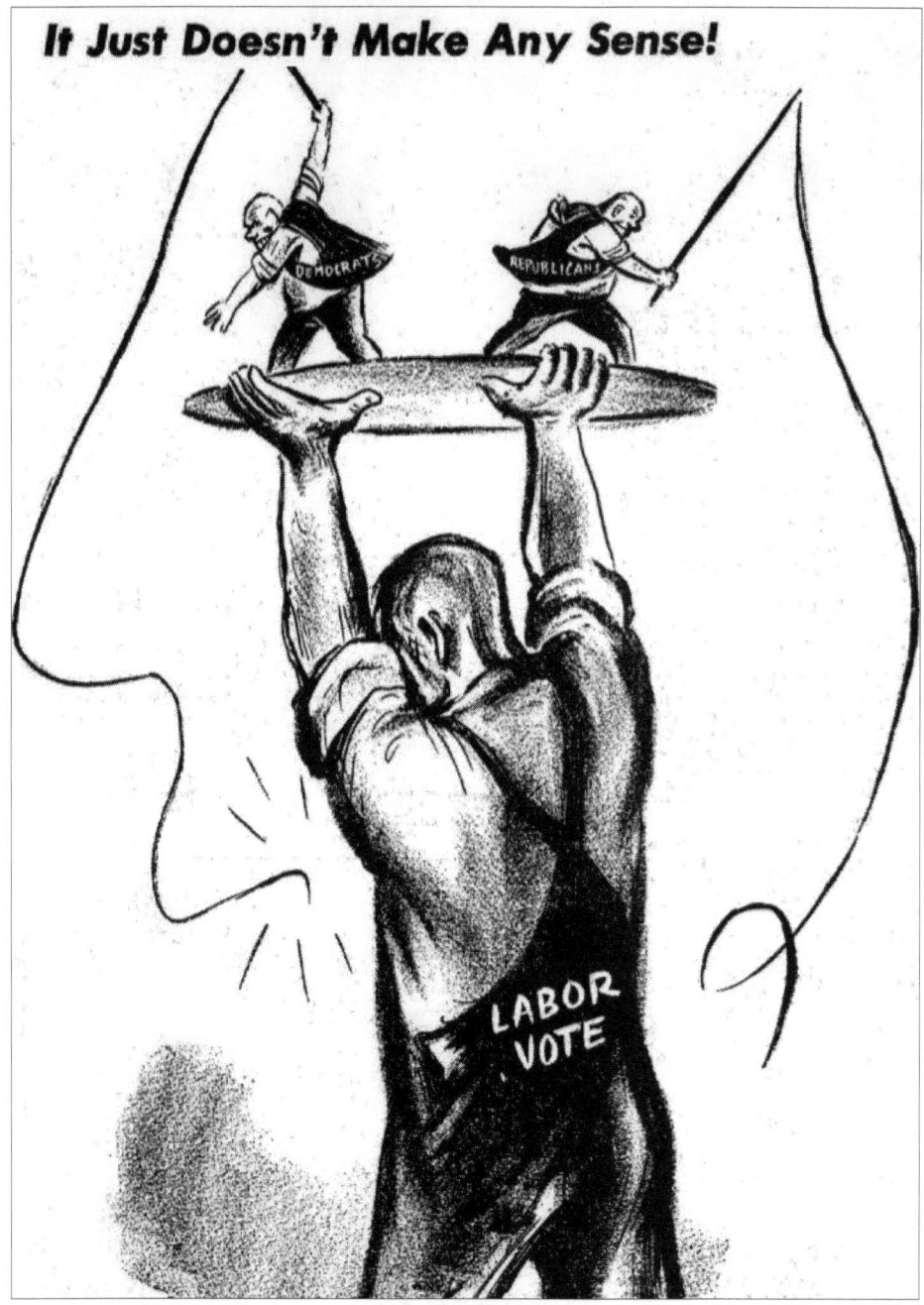

10 November 1947

23 August 1948. From the late 1930s the Trotskyists campaigned for the US unions to follow the example of the British unions at the beginning of the 20th century and form a trade union based Labour Party. Within such a structure the militants would argue for revolutionary socialist politics and perspectives.

24 May 1948

30 June 1947

14 July 1947. William Green and Philip Murray were the president of the two US union confederations, the AFL and the CIO.

Above: 31 July 1944. The elephant and the donkey are emblems of the US Republican Party (GOP) and Democrats. Right: The sinking boat is inscribed "Democratic-Labour Coalition".

19 June 1944. The elephant and the donkey are emblems of the US Republican and Democratic Parties.

4 Proposals to the working class

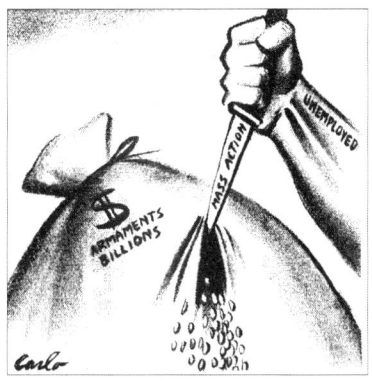

"To face reality squarely; not to seek the line of least resistance; to call things by their right names; to speak the truth to the masses, no matter how bitter it may be; not to fear obstacles; to be true in little things as in big ones; to base one's programme on the logic of the class struggle; to be bold when the hour for action arrives – these are the rules..." — Leon Trotsky, The Death Agony of Capitalism and the Tasks of the Fourth International

Previous page: 7 April 1939. Above: 7 August 1944. In 1938 the Founding Congress of the Fourth International adopted a program entitled The Death Agony of Capitalism and the Tasks of the Fourth International, commonly known as the Transitional Programme. It contained "demands" worked out for a variety of exigencies, some of which are expounded in the cartoons in this section.

Above: 4 February 1946. Right: 31 December 1945.

Who Says It's None of Our Business!

Above: 27 July 1946. Below: 25 March 1946.

7 January 1939

Above: 18 February 1946. Right: 14 Oct 1946. Agreements by which wages were tied to rise in line with prices were called "escalator clauses" or the "sliding scale of wages"

Above: 24 September 1945.
Right: 28 July 1947. The weapon is a 24 hour general strike.

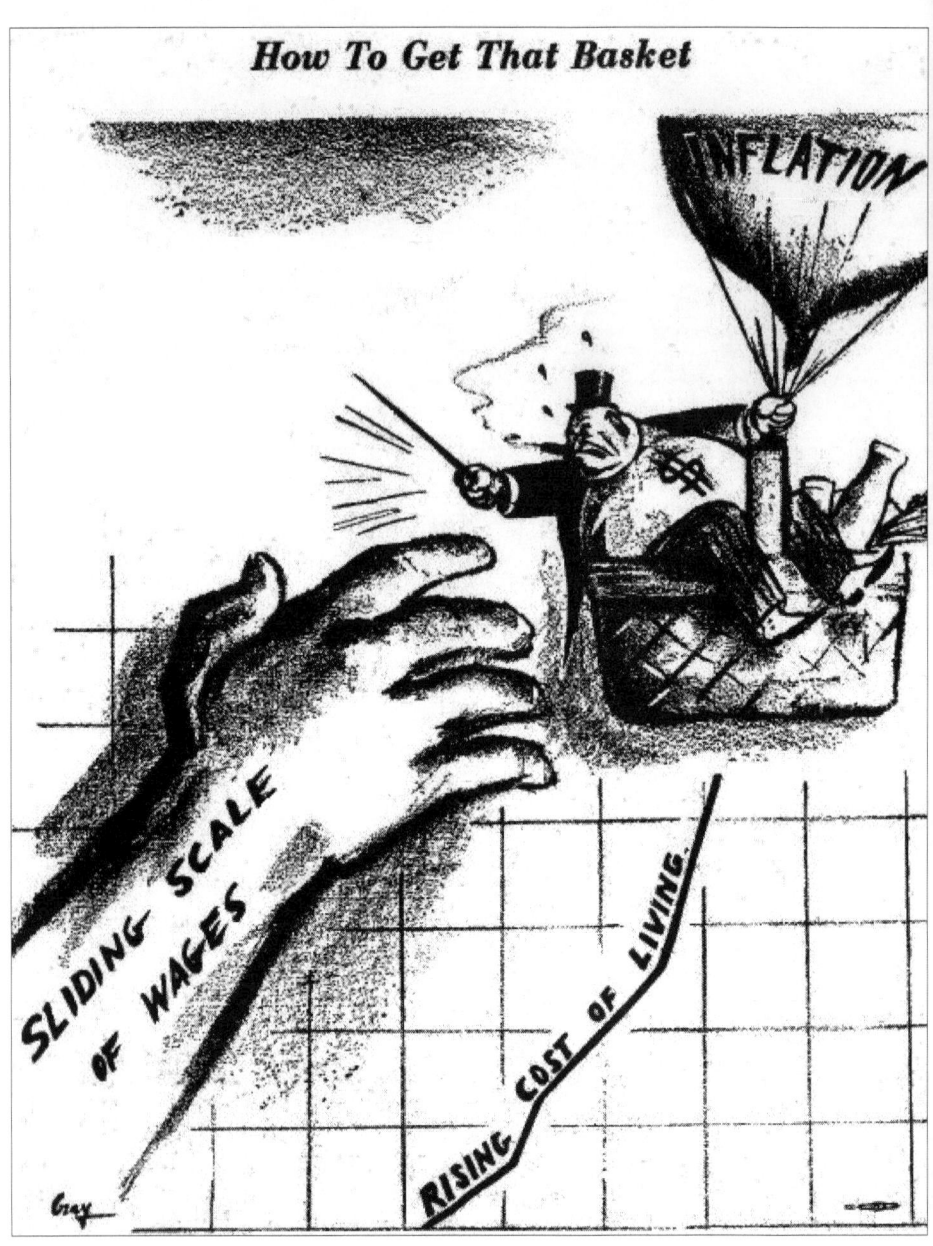

27 July 1946. Consumer price inflation ran high in the USA from mid-1946 to the end of 1948, with a peak of 19.7% per year in March 1947. The "sliding scale of wages" was a measure by which wages would automatically rise in line with prices.

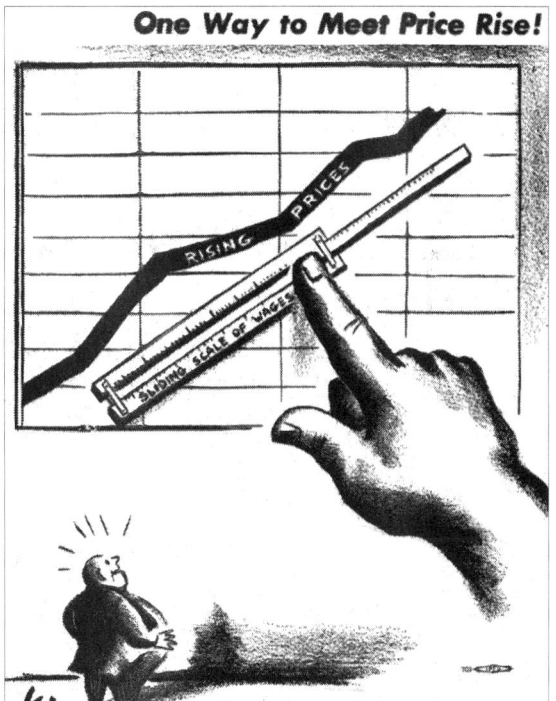

Above: 7 June 1943.
Right: 5 May 1947.

2 August 1943

Above: 8 September 1947. Right: 3 April 1943. The rising or sliding scale meant a deal under which wages rose automatically when prices rose.

7 May 1938. The cop's uniform is inscribed "Hague machine". Frank Hague was the notoriously thuggish mayor of Jersey City and influential in the Democratic Party nationally.

Above: 28 January 1939. Right: 10 August 1940. The flag is inscribed "Union Local [Branch] 232".

23 June 1939. The scurrying figures are inscribed "Bosses", "Fascism", and "Hagueism" (after Frank Hague, the notoriously thuggish mayor of New Jersey and a leading figure in the Democratic Party).

Above: 21 December 1946. Right: 25 October 1948, as wartime rent controls were eased.

Above: 1 September 1947, as wartime rent controls were eased. Right: 25 March 1946

Above: 19 May 1947. Willie Francis, an African American, had been sentenced to death at the age of 16. The electric chair failed to kill first time round. After legal appeals, the state electrocuted him again, killing him that time. A March on Washington Movement, demanding an end to racial discrimination, existed from 1941 to 1947, though it never actually marched on Washington. Right: 24 May 1947, campaigning against the Taft-Hartley law.

Above: 26 May 1947. Right: 7 June 1947. From the period of the battle against the Taft-Hartley law.

Above: 16 June 1947. The figures begging the worker to write to Congress are union leaders William Green and Philip Murray. Below: 31 Dec 1956.

23 December 1946. A rent-freeze law applied in the USA during World War Two, but rent controls were successively eased after the war.

5
Jim Crow: fighting racism

"Labour cannot emancipate itself in the white skin where in the black it is branded" — Marx, Capital volume 1

Four Freedoms for America!

FREEDOM FROM:
1 – LYNCHING
2 – INDUSTRIAL DISCRIMINATION
3 – POLL TAXES
4 – JIM CROWISM

Carlo

Previous page: 13 May 1957. Above: 11 January 1943. President Roosevelt declared "Four Freedoms" (not including freedom from racism) in January 1941 as part of the preparation for the USA entering World War 2.

Lynching of African Americans was less common by 1946 than it had been in the 1920s, when over 50 African Americans were lynched each year, but still at least six were lynched in 1946.

21 December 1942

The Negro Soldier's Bitterest Enemy

Above: 27 April 1946. The US armed forces were racially segregated in World War 2, and were not fully integrated until 1954. Right: 2 June 1947. Racists charged with lynching Willie Earle in South Carolina had been acquitted without even calling any defence witnesses.

Above: 12 Sep 1955. Emmett Till was a 14-year-old Chicago boy on his first visit to the South, for a holiday with a relative. Accused of whistling at a young woman serving in a store, he was kidnapped, horribly beaten and murdered. His body was hidden in a swamp. When his body was recovered, terribly mutilated, his relatives put it on the show in an open coffin. 50,000 people went to view it. The murder roused bitter anger all over America and across the world. Two white men were tried and acquitted by a local jury. They later admitted their guilt. The Emmett Till case contributed to militancy then beginning among American black people. A few weeks later Rosa Parks refused to give up her seat on a bus to a white man and triggered a whole new phase in the struggle for African American civil rights.

Caught in the Act

Above: 9 March 1953. Right: 5 March 1951. John Derrick was shot by cops in New York in Dec 1950.

Welcome Home!

"WHIP HAND"

In the Camp of "Democracy"

Previous page: 23 Sep 1946 (top), 7 May 1956 (left), 6 Oct 1941 (right). Above: 12 Jan 1942. The USO was and is a charity set up by religious and other groups with government aid to provide recreation for US troops. The Philadelphia USO centre banned African-American troops. Right: 10 August 1942.

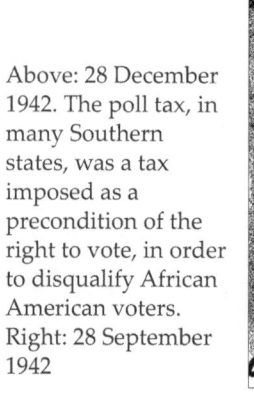

Above: 28 December 1942. The poll tax, in many Southern states, was a tax imposed as a precondition of the right to vote, in order to disqualify African American voters. Right: 28 September 1942

"No, I don't practice discrimination, but how many janitor jobs do you think there are round here?"

Above: 8 September 1945.
Right: 24 February 1947

Above: 11 October 1954. The figure in Ku Klux Klan costume is inscribed "School Segregation". In May 1954 the Supreme Court had ruled school segregation illegal. Right: 9 June 1947.

9 August 1948. The Southern Democrats, or Dixiecrats, were racist, and blocked anti-racist legislation by filibustering, or talking it out, in Congress. The close link between the Democratic Party and Southern racism ended only in the Reagan era.

June 1923: "The Exodus from Dixie" [the South]. During and after World War 1 many African Americans moved to the north.

"Not wanted" (1920s)

Above: 26 June 1926: "Which way now?". Below: 29 November 1927: "You can't vote, yer too ignorant".

6
Roosevelt and the New Deal

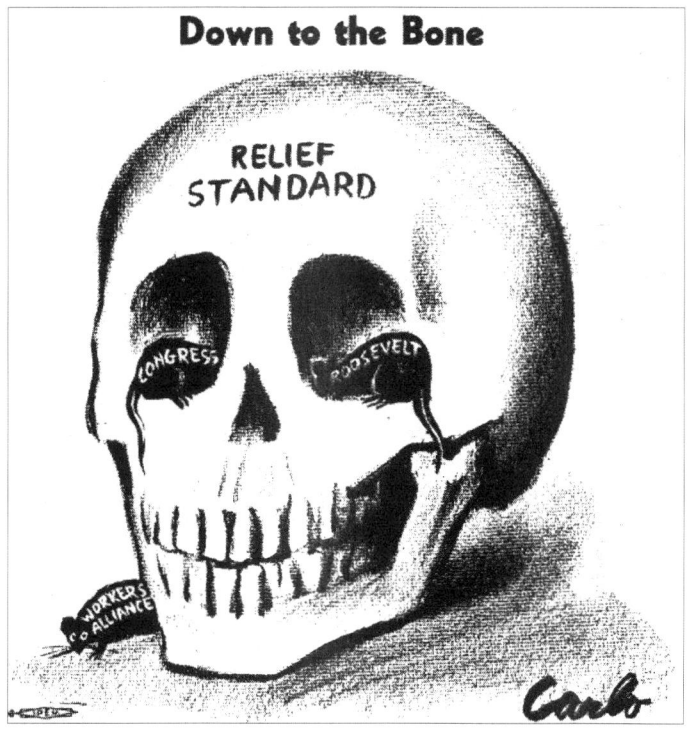

"The New Deal, despite its first period of pretentious resoluteness, represents but a special form of political perplexity, possible only in a country where the bourgeoisie has succeeded in accumulating incalculable wealth"
— Leon Trotsky

Previous page: 9 June 1939. Unemployment in the USA was over 14% every year from 1931 to 1940, and 17% in 1939. Above: 11 July 1939. "Tories" in the USA originally meant people who supported Britain against the USA's war of independence, but was later used to mean traditionalist conservatives more generally. Roosevelt presented himself as hostile to such people — but it was mainly pretence and empty demagogy. The economic vested interests, the "Tories", retained what they had.

6 September 1939. The figure at the microphone is President Franklin D Roosevelt. "Wilson" was Woodrow Wilson, who was re-elected president in November 1916 on a promise to keep the USA out of World War 1, and then took the USA into the war on 6 April 1917

11 November 1940. Roosevelt was first elected president in 1932, and then re-elected for second, third, and fourth terms before dying in April 1945. The WPA was the Works Progress Administration, an agency set up to manage public works programmes. Home Relief was the major welfare benefits programme under Roosevelt's New Deal. Roosevelt introduced military conscription (the "draft") in September 1940, over a year before the USA entered World War 2.

5 May 1939. Woodrow Wilson, re-elected president in 1916 on a promise to keep the USA out of World War 1, took the USA into the war in April 1917.

Above: 20 May 1940. All the figures represent President Franklin D Roosevelt. Below: 6 January 1941.

7
Stalinism

"The present purge draws between Bolshevism and Stalinism not simply a bloody line but a whole river of blood. The annihilation of all the older generation of Bolsheviks... shows not only a political but a thoroughly physical incompatibility between Bolshevism and Stalinism" — Leon Trotsky, Stalinism and Bolshevism

Stalinism

The Communist International was set up in 1919 to organise a world revolution. With the Stalinist counterrevolution in Russia, the Communist International became a tool of the bureaucracy, used as a pressure point for Russia's interests and policies all over the world. This involved sometimes spectacular shifts of policy by these parties.

From before the Seventh World Congress of the Communist International (the last, in 1935), the Stalinists all over the world campaigned for a war of the "democracies" (which included Russia, of course) against fascist Germany. They campaigned for a cross-class "democratic alliance" in a "People's Front".

In Britain this came to mean advocacy of a coalition government between the Labour Party, the Liberal party, and "progressive Tories". The Stalinists opposed the Labour Party when, with victory in Europe in May 1945, it broke the wartime coalition with the Tories and fought for a majority in the subsequent General Election, the one that produced a majority Labour government.

In America, the Popular Front meant support for President Roosevelt and opposition to an independent party of labour.

In Spain, the Stalinists suppressed the workers' revolution that had effective power in parts of the Spanish state. The murdered anarchists, Trotskyists, independent socialists such as the POUM.

When Stalin and Hitler signed a pact in August 1939, the loyal Stalinists turned themselves on their heads politically and became advocates of peace on Hitler's terms. The Stalinists in occupied France were allowed to publish a paper, which made routine propaganda for the Hitler camp against the "imperialists" such as Great Britain. In Mexico the Communist Party denounced the "Jewish Trotskyists".

When Hitler invaded Russia in June 1941, the Communist Parties switched to advocating war on Hitler. In the US, in particular, between the invasion of Russia in June 1941 and Pearl Harbour in December 1941, the Stalinists were blatant warmongers. The easiest access to that now is by way of songs of that period by Woody Guthrie and Pete Seeger, such as "The Reuben James".

When America entered the war the Stalinists became strikebreakers, informants to the police, advocates and organisers of vigilante action against the Trotskyists and others.

The Communist International was formally abolished in May 1943.

The US Communist Party leader Earl Browder, became an out and out advocate of capitalism. Anticipating a continuation of the US-Russian alliance, in 1944 he liquidated the Communist Party into something called the Communist Political Association. After the Communist Party was reconstituted in 1945, at Russian diktat, Browder was demoted and eventually expelled.

The USSR

31 October 1939.

Above: 29 January 1938. Below: 4 December 1937

The Stalintern

Above: 17 August 1935. The 7th Congress of the Comintern in Jul-Aug 1935 had codified the "Popular Front" policy. The Comintern went over to supporting the more prosperous bourgeois states, the bourgeois democracies. Below: 29 May 1943. The Comintern was dissolved on 22 May.

The League of Nations imposed economic sanctions on Italy in 1935-6, when it invaded Ethiopia. Revolutionary socialists supported Ethiopian resistance to Italian conquest but opposed the sanctions (which did not in fact impede the conquest) as a step to inter-imperialist war. Below: 22 June 1953

The Judgment of History

22 October 1938. The Trotskyist movement formally declared itself "the Fourth International" in September 1938. The First International, in which Marx and Engels had been active, operated from 1864 into the 1870s. The Second International was founded in 1889 and collapsed politically at the start of World War One in August 1914. The Third International was the Communist International, founded in 1919, but converted by Stalin into something quite different by the 1930s, and formally wound up in 1943.

The Popular Front

14 March 1939. The Popular Front was the policy, codified in 1935, by which the Comintern was directed to support bourgeois democratic forces thought likely to help the USSR against Germany.

14 February 1939.

The Spanish Revolution

3 March 1939. The Spanish Civil War (1936-9) ended in victory for the fascists led by General Franco on 1 April 1939. When Franco first launched his military coup against the Republic, in July 1936, it had been pushed back in a mobilisation in which workers armed themselves and took control of production. Stalinists and bourgeois Republican politicians suppressed the independent workers' mobilisation by mid-1937.

The Spanish "United Front"

Above: 28 May 1938: the corpses are inscribed "Political Opponents".

Right: 20 Nov 1937: the corpse is inscribed "Revolutionists". The Stalinist secret police (GPU) was active in Spain and killed many revolutionaries.

28 February 1939. As Franco advanced, the Spanish Republican (People's Front) government fled to France, president Manuel Azana in February 1939 and prime minister Juan Negrin in March. "No Pasaran" ("they [fascists] shall not pass") had been a catchcry of the Republic (and the Stalinists especially).

The Moscow Trials

16 July 1938. The third of the Moscow show trials in which Stalin had got most of the remaining old Bolshevik leaders convicted, on trumped-up charges of collaboration with fascism, and then killed, was in March 1938. The previous ones were in August 1936 and January 1937. They were the highest-profile events in the Great Terror, from 1934 to 1938, in which Stalin massacred oppositionists, and even large numbers of the Stalin faction. Leon Trotsky was "found guilty" in the 1936 Moscow Trial, and murdered by a Stalinist agent in 1940. It was a Stalinist catchphrase that the USSR would "catch and outstrip" the West

18 December 1937.

Stains That Won't Come Off

The Real Moscow Defendant

Above: 12 March 1938. Right: 19 March 1938. In December 1936, at the height of the Great Terror, the USSR had adopted a new constitution which it called "the most democratic in the world". The small figures in the top cartoon are US Stalinists; in the bottom one, Stalin.

15 May 1943. "Mission to Moscow" was a US film made in 1943, based on a book by a former US Ambassador to Moscow, which tried to justify the Moscow Trials.

24 May 1943. The small figure is Earl Browder, then leader of the US Communist Party. "Mission to Moscow" was a 1943 film made by the Warner Brothers studio (and, on some accounts, at US government request). It depicted the Moscow trials in Stalin's point of view. Allegedly based on a memoir by the plutocrat, and former US Ambassador in Moscow, Joseph E Davies, the film opened with an appearance by Davies himself assuring the audience of the truth of the fantastic rigmarole written by Stalin's script writers for the Moscow Trials. The film caused outrage among politically literate people in the USA. Pickets were organised at cinemas at which it was being shown. Howard Koch, who wrote "Mission to Moscow", also co-wrote the well-known and still very popular film "Casablanca": both were produced by Warner Bros, and both were directed by Michael Curtiz.

The murder of Leon Trotsky

1 May 1944.

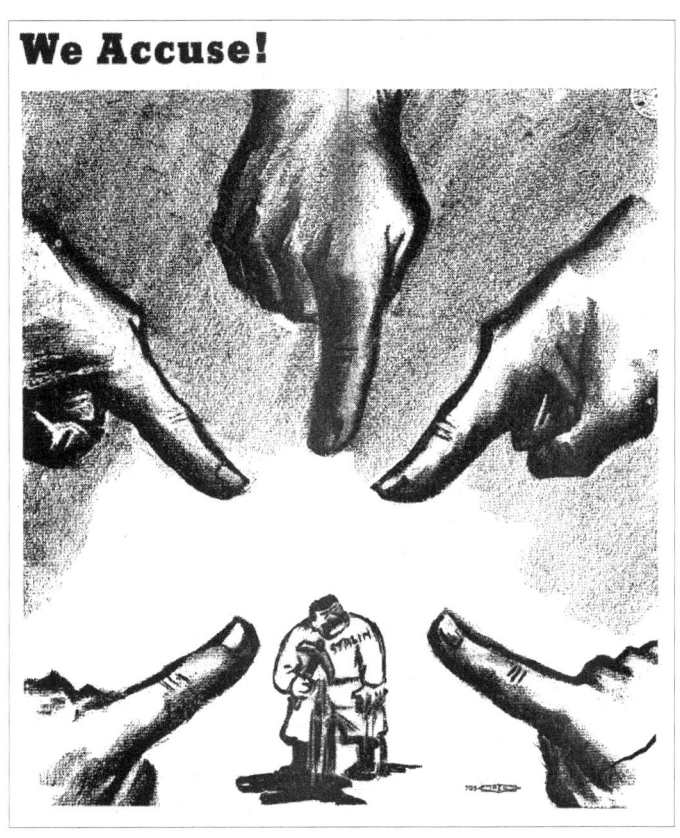

Above: 2 September 1940. Below: 8 March 1947.

Above: 26 August 1940.
Right: 24 August 1940. The two US Trotskyist papers report the murder of Trotsky by a Stalinist agent on 20 August 1940.

Parrot party: the CPUSA

A Mask for Every Season

After the German invasion of the USSR in June 1941, the Communist Parties everywhere supported the Allied governments in World War 2. The Communist Party of the USA, newly "respectable", grew fast. In January 1944 it decided that relations between the USSR and US governments were so good that it should dissolve in favour of a looser "Communist Political Association". As the Cold War began, that decision was reversed in July 1945 and the CP USA was reconstituted. Changing masks, and changing again, in a perpetual masquerade, was the policy of the "Communist" Parties, steered by Stalin's often-changed domestic and international policy.

The United Front from Below

2 October 1937. The small figure is Earl Browder, leader of the Communist Party USA. The hatred engendered by the Communist Party's role during the war – at one time it advocated that striking miners should be conscripted and forced to work at bayonet point – pre-dated the post-war McCarthyite campaign against the Communist Party, though it contributed to the speedy isolation of the Communist Party in that period. Both sections of Trotskyists, Cannonites and Shachtmanites in equal measure, hated the Stalinist party, and that pervades these cartoons. "The United Front from Below" had been a Stalinist catchphrase in 1928-34, when they effectively refused to ally with social democrats against fascists by saying they would unite only "from below".

Above: 9 October 1937. Below: 16 October 1937. Communist Party USA leader Earl Browder is shown as a performing seal for capitalists. singing the US national anthem, "The Star-Spangled Banner", which starts: "Oh, say, can you see..."

11 December 1937. Patrick Corcoran was a Teamster union activist, in a Trotskyist-led local in Minneapolis, who was mysteriously murdered on 11 November 1937, it was thought by right-wing pro-boss gangsters.

8 January 1938. The small figure is CP USA leader Earl Browder; the tank driver is inscribed "Capitalism" and driving to World War 2.

Above: 21 May 1938. Below: 4 June 1938. The car (above) is labelled "United Auto Workers"; the hitch-hiking "CP" vagabond figure is holding a knife inscribed "End Factionalism".

13 August 1938. Right: 27 May 1944. Wall St, in New York, symbolises capitalist high finance.

Above: 19 Nov 1938. Below: 10 Mar 1939. On 20 February 1939, the SWP led a 50,000 strong protest at a fascist meeting at Madison Square Garden. The CP boycotted the protest. Max Shachtman was the main SWP speaker at the protest, which was comparable to the famous 1936 Battle of Cable St in London

26 May 1939. "Gyp joint" meant a bar or gambling den that charged excessive prices for shoddy goods. In 1939 the memoirs of a defecting Stalinist agent, Walter Krivitsky, had revealed that Stalin referred to the Communist International, which he controlled, as "the gyp joint". The Workers' Alliance was a Communist Party front. In the mid and late 1930s, and until 1947-8, the CP supported Roosevelt and the Democratic Party, and opposed moves to independent working-class politics in the USA.

20 October 1941. The name of the CP USA's newspaper was the *Daily Worker*, but it was very different from the *Daily Worker* of the 1920s. After the USSR entered the war with Hitler's invasion of the USSR in June 1941, the Communist Party opposed strikes, and where it could engaged in direct strike-breaking. It fomented a lynch-mob attitude towards strikers.

5 October 1942. The figure telling the worker squashed by capitalist industry to be quiet is inscribed "Stalinists". The Communist Parties in Allied countries opposed strikes after the USSR entered World War 2.

Above: 17 January 1944. The small figure is CP USA leader Browder. The elephant and donkey are emblems of the US Republican and Democratic Parties. Below: 12 June 1944.

Above: 9 July 1945, when the CP USA reconstituted itself after formally dissolving the party in 1944. The label on the parrot says "Communist Party". Below: 15 July 1944. "Goons" means thugs.

ONE TURN TOO MANY

9 July 1945: Browder was scapegoated for the 1944 dissolution of the CP and expelled. Right: 17 June 1944

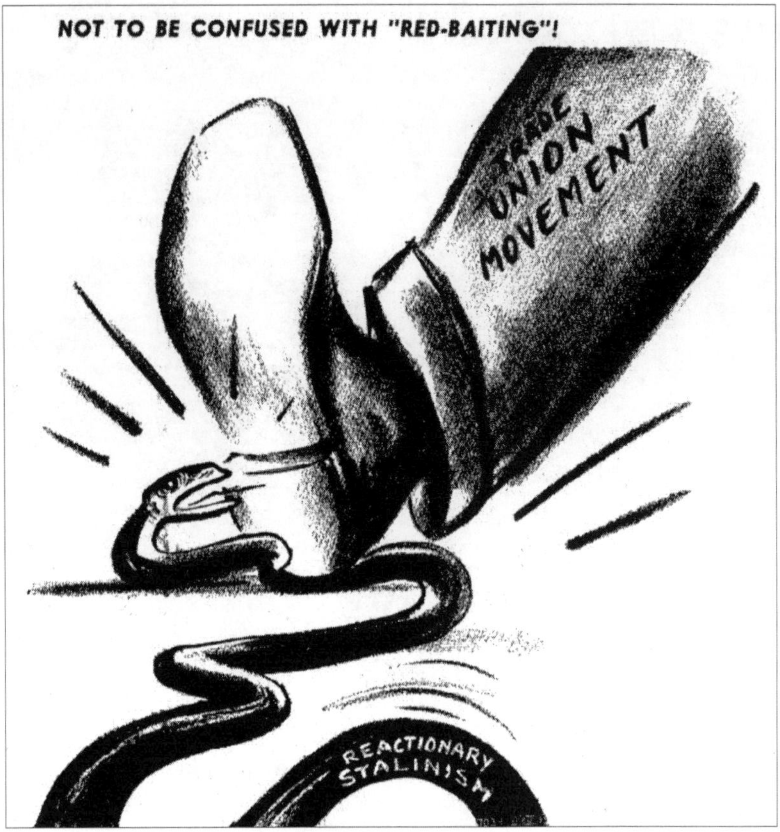

Above: 1 Dec 1947. Below: 6 October 1939

The Stalin-Hitler pact

6 September 1939.

15 October 1938. At the end of September 1938 France and Britain signed an agreement with Hitler allowing him to seize large parts of Czechoslovakia. Stalin, seeing his hopes that France and Britain would protect him against Hitler, was spurred to the search for other options which led to the Stalin-Hitler pact of August 1939.

Champions of Peace and Democracy!

German-Soviet Pact

Carlo

Socialism In One Country Goes International

Above: 1 October 1939, referring to the pact between Stalin and Hitler made in August 1939. Right: 27 Oct 1939. The small figure is Stalin.

"A Matter of Taste"---Molotov

Change Your Partners!

25 Nov 1940. USSR minister Molotov, when signing the 1939 pact with Hitler, said that "fascism is a matter of taste".
Right: 29 August 1939. The dancing figures are Hitler and Stalin; the cherub is CP USA leader Browder; the rejected partner is labelled "Democratic Front".

8
Fascism

"There are among the Communist officials not a few cowardly careerists and fakers who... spout ultraradical phrases and... get their passports ready. Worker-Communists, you are hundreds of thousands, millions; you cannot leave for anyplace; there are not enough passports for you. Should fascism come to power, it will ride over your skulls and spines like a terrific tank. Your salvation lies in merciless struggle. And only a fighting unity with the Social Democratic workers can bring victory. Make haste, worker-Communists, you have very little time left!" –
Leon Trotsky, For a Workers' United Front Against Fascism, 1931

Native fascism

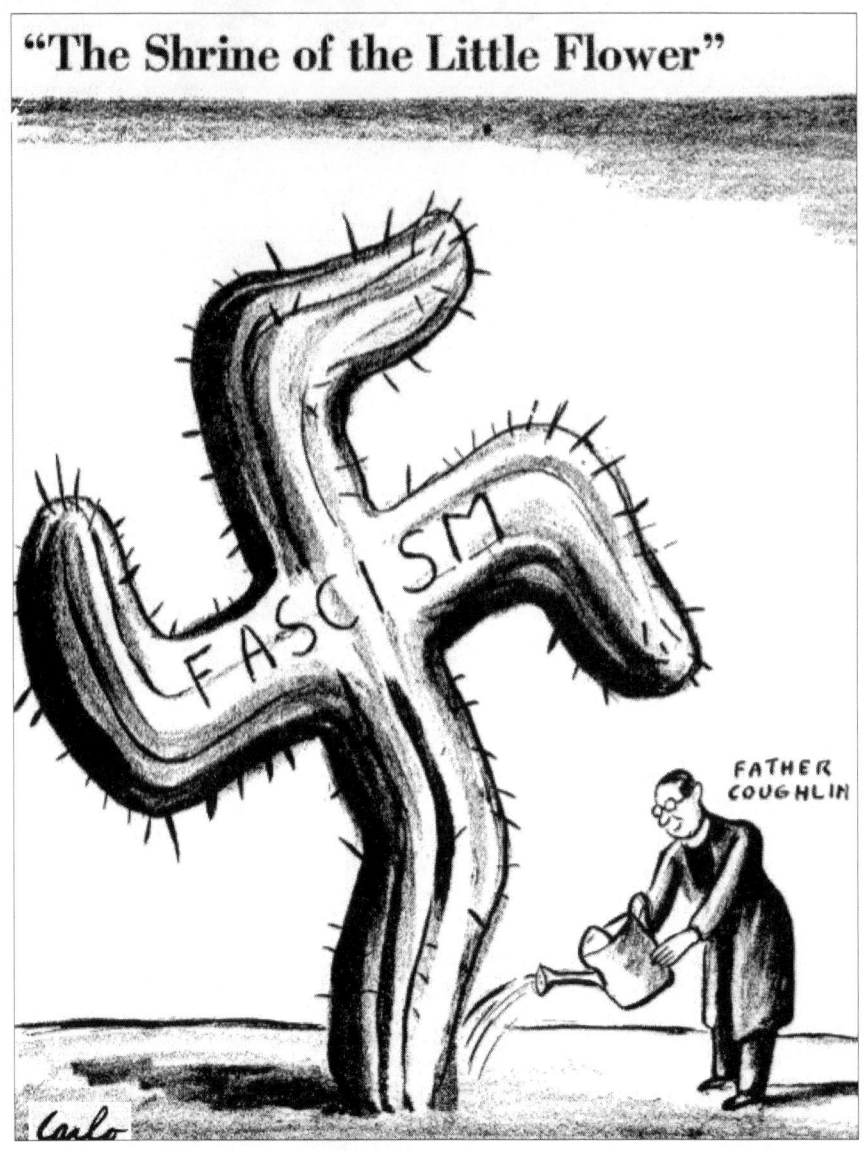

Charles Coughlin was a fascist leader in the USA in the 1930s and Catholic priest at the Shrine of the Little Flower church in Michigan. "The Little Flower" was a 19th century nun made a Catholic saint in 1925. Previous page: 30 March 1946.

Above: 18 August 1939. The small figure is "the radio priest" Coughlin, leader of the fascist "Union for Social Justice". Right: 16 April 1942. The figures round the flag are "Coughlinites" and "Silver Shirts", another fascist grouping.

Above: 4 July 1939. The small figure is the fascist leader and Catholic priest Charles Coughlin, whose movement was called the Union for Social Justice. Right: 17 March 1939.

Above: 7 July 1939. The small figures are inscribed "capitalist cops", "Stalinists", and "liberals". Right: 14 July 1939. The Trotskyists helped organise workers' defence guards in some areas which did beat back the fascists.

Hitlerism

17 December 1938. The League of Nations (forerunner of the UN) was supposed to organise "collective security", and in the later 1930s, until August 1939, the Stalinists appealed to France and Britain to organise that "collective security".

Above: 22 September 1941. ight: 13 July 1940. In June 1940 the French government made a deal with Hitler for part of France to come under Nazi occupation and the rest under a compliant French government.

Catholic reaction

14 March 1949. In 1949 Cardinal Spellman attacked grave diggers striking at a Catholic cemetery and organised strike breakers. Right: 1 August 1949

Above: 12 October 1927. Below: 11 October 1927. There was an armed Catholic rebellion against the radical secularist Mexican government in 1927-8.

Anti-semitism and other bigotries

26 November 1938. Especially after Kristallnacht in November 1938, Jews from Germany and Europe sought refuge in the USA. The vast majority were turned away.

3 December 1938. The small figures are labelled "German refugees". Anti-Semitism was strong in the USA. There were "quotas" of Jews for colleges. In responses published in mid-1945 to a questionnaire about the training of dentists in America, a majority of American dentists expressed satisfaction at the state of dentist training schools in America — except that there were too many Jews in the dental colleges. The revelation of what had happened in the Nazi death camps coincided with a spate of attacks on Jewish people all over the USA. Right: 14 Oct 1946.

Above: 24 August 1946. From August 1946 to January 1949 Britain ran internment camps in Cyprus (then British-ruled) for Jews caught trying to flee to Palestine. During the war, so as to try to placate Arab opinion, Britain blocked all but a trickle of Jews into Palestine. Large numbers of Jews were kept in "displaced persons'" camps in Europe until 1948. Israel was established, and Britain lost control of immigration into Palestine, in May 1948.

Top: 11 November 1946. The small figure is prime minister Clement Attlee. Right: 22 June 1946. Left: 19 May 1945

31 January 1949.

9
World War

"The immediate cause of the present war is the rivalry between the old wealthy colonial empires, Great Britain and France, and the belated imperialist plunderers, Germany and Italy... Caught off guard, the British government first attempted to buy its way out of war by concessions at the expense of others. But this policy was short lived. Thus the 'new era of peace' proclaimed by Chamberlain in October 1938 led within a few months to the most terrible of all wars..." — Manifesto of the Fourth International on the Imperialist War and the Proletarian Revolution

On the road to war

23 Oct 1937: figures are labelled pacifist, reformist, Stalinist, etc.
Previous page: 4 April 1939.

"When?"

Above: 29 September 1939. Below: 26 September 1939.

The Capitalist Answer

"Everybody Must Sacrifice Something!"

Above: 8 July 1940. Right: 15 September 1941

Above: 28 October 1940. Below: 17 March 1941.

5 May 1941. The USA's "Neutrality Patrol" in 1939-41 was de facto help by the US Navy to the British Navy in convoying merchant shipping across the Atlantic Ocean. In July-August 1941 the US froze Japanese assets in the US and established an embargo on oil and gasoline exports to Japan: at the time more than 80 percent of Japan's oil at the time came from the United States. The US was clearly moving towards war well before Japan retaliated by bombing the US naval base at Pearl Harbour in Hawaii.

The World War

28 March 1939. The top-hatted figure is inscribed "Democracies".

25 May 1942

Above: 7 November 1939. Below: 6 June 1939.

Right: 15 December 1939.
Below: 29 December 1941.

The Ultimate Victor?

Above: 21 May 1945. Below: 19 August 1946.

Taking the profit out of war

13 November 1937. In many countries, between the two World Wars Armistice Day was marked on 11 November itself (not on the nearest Sunday, as now), with a two-minute pause and silence at 11am when most people were at work.

Above: 11 August 1939. Below: 15 July 1940.

Right: 12 August 1940. Below: 12 September 1939.

Above: 27 July 1942. Below: 5 April 1943.

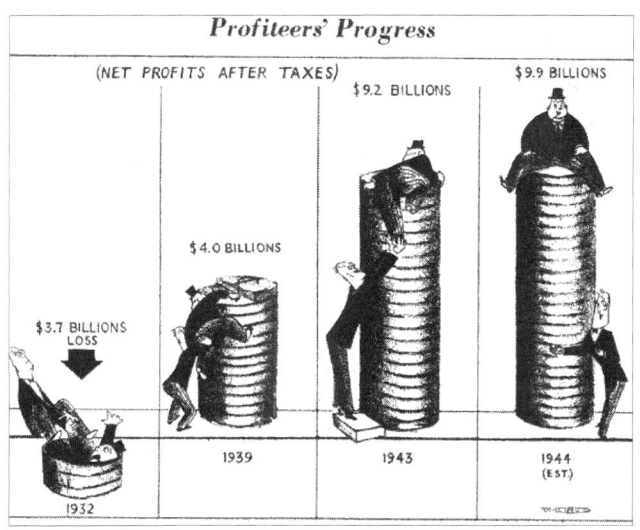

Above: 11 March 1944. Below: 29 July 1946.

June 1927: "A Government-fed baby"

17 Dec 1927: "I just had lunch with the President".

Labour in the war

27 June 1939.

1 December 1941

Another Battle for Freedom!

Above: 18 January 1943. Right: 14 December 1942.

29 March 1943.

3 May 1943. "No-strike pledge: When the United States entered the war in December 1941, the leaders of both the AFL and the CIO pledged that there should be no strikes or walkouts for the duration of the war. Strikes happened nevertheless.

Democracy on the Home Front

THE RIGHT TO STRIKE

CONNALLY BILL

Some Unfinished Business

Above: 21 June 1943. The anti-strike Connally Bill was passed by Congress in June 1943, though vetoed by Roosevelt. Right: 14 May 1945. The prostrate figures on the right are labelled "Hitler" and "Mussolini"; the figure making off to the left, "Capitalism".

A Twist of the Wrist Would Put Them to Rout!

"The Greatest Liberal of Them All"

Above: 17 July 1944. Below: 20 January 1945. Union leaders made a "no strike" pledge in the war. In 1944 Roosevelt introduced a "labour draft" which in the end did not come to much.

3 September 1945.

10
Civil liberty

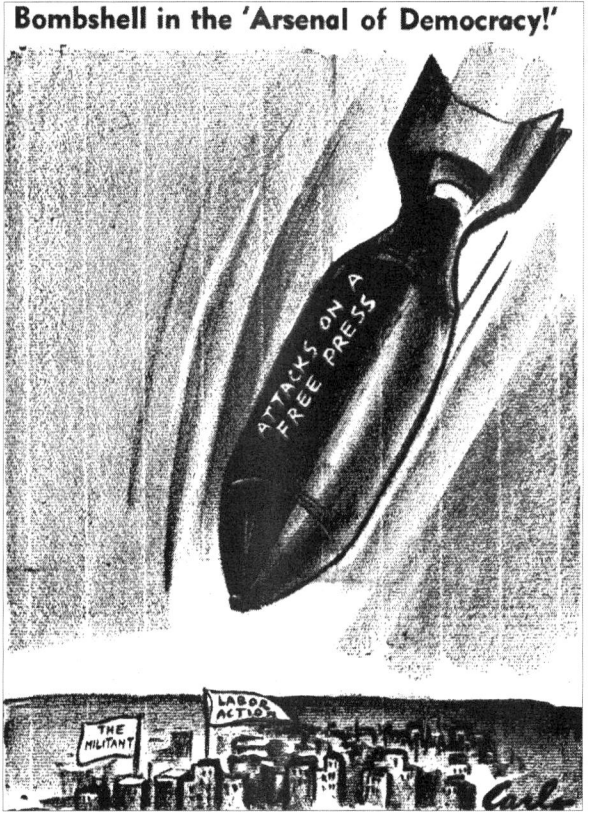

"The Fourth International does not discard the programme of the old 'minimal' demands to the degree to which these have preserved at least part of their vital forcefulness. Indefatigably, it defends the democratic rights and social conquests of the toilers" — Leon Trotsky, The Death Agony of Capitalism

23 May 1939. Previous page: 8 February 1943. In 1943 the US authorities cancelled cheaper mailing rates for the Trotskyist papers, *Labor Action* and *The Militant,* which depended for much of their circulation on postal subscriptions.

The Real Blackout

The Same Beast

Above: 3 June 1940. Right: 13 October 1939. Basing themselves on the World War 1 record, the socialists expected fiercer repression in wartime than actually happened.

The Blitz on the Home Front!

26 October 1942.

19 March 1945. The figure in the poster "trying to enslave" the worker is a typical wartime racist Japanese stereotype.

Above: 18 December 1943. The Smith Act of 1940 made it a crime to advocate the overthrow of the US government; Trotskyists were jailed under it. Right: 1 February 1947.

Above: 2 July 1951. Below: 10 December 1956. The anti-strike Taft-Hartley law of 1947 help to beat down the working-class militancy which had run high in 1946-7.

Above: 25 July 1949. The rats are inscribed "FBI", "Tom Clark" (then US Attorney General), "Stalinists". Below: 11 July 1949. Even after it was under attack the CP USA did not support civil rights for Trotskyists.

The Minneapolis Case

11 July 1941. In June 1941, the Minneapolis office of one Trotskyist group, the SWP, was raided by cops. Trotskyist leaders of the Teamsters Union in Minneapolis were charged under the Smith Act. They and other Trotskyists, 18 in all, were jailed.

Conspiracy in Minneapolis!

Above: 3 November 1941. The thugs in waiting are inscribed "Tobin" (right-wing union leader), "Roosevelt", and "bosses". Right: 8 November 1941.

Above: 27 October 1941. The judge's documents are inscribed "Minn[eapolis] indictments". Below: 17 June 1944.

12 June 1941. Local 544 was the Trotskyist-led Teamster branch in Minneapolis. Tobin was the right-wing national leader of the Teamsters' union. Stassen was Governor of Minnesota; Kline was mayor of Minneapolis.

Above: 10 June 1944. 18 Trotskyists were jailed under the Smith Act from December 1941. Below: 25 March 1944. On the orders of the trial judge, the police burned books seized in raids on the Minneapolis SWP office.

Sacco and Vanzetti

22 August 1927. Nicola Sacco and Bartolomeo Vanzetti were Italian-born anarchists framed on charges of murder in 1920 and, despite a big campaign by the international labour movement, killed by the US state on 23 August 1927.

19 August 1927

11 Jul 1927 (above); 4 Nov 1927. "While the working class sleeps"

11 August 1927: "Is this the emblem?". The statue of judicial murder here parodies the Statue of Liberty.

22 July 1927: "Have A Seat".

11
The war is over

"The partitioning of Germany, the annexation of territories, the plundering of machines from factories, requisitioning of all types, the confiscation of arms, deportations, the evacuation of millions from their native homes, the hunger blockade, reparations running into billions – this is the 'peace' given the German people under the excuse that they are collectively guilty. German working people! In this situation, we, the International Communists, feel obligated to stand by you with all the power and conviction of our class solidarity. Understand that we are not Social Democrats – who with cowardly opportunism act as agents of Anglo-American and French imperialism in Western Germany. Understand also that we are not Stalinists – who shout still louder under Russian command in declaring the German people guilty and who hail the annexations in the East. We are Communists in the spirit of Lenin" — Manifesto by European sections of the Fourth International, late 1945

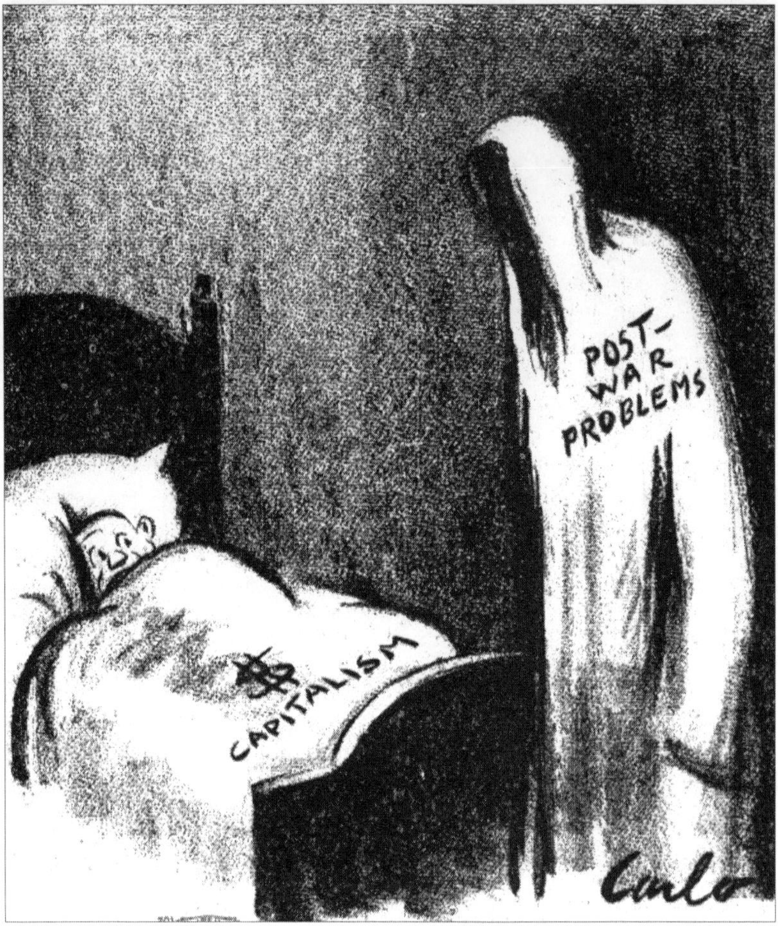

12 May 1947. Socialists and many others expected economic chaos after 1945 as after 1918; and in fact economic recovery was wobbly, and economic devastation in Europe grievous, until the Korean War boom of 1950-3, which then proved to be the start of two decades of rapid and relatively stable capitalist growth. Right: 29 September 1945.

The victors

26 March 1945. Stalin's whip is inscribed "Enslavement for Germany". Churchill is carrying a cudgel inscribed "Greece", where the British army was suppressing Stalinist-led rebellion. In 1944 Roosevelt had announced a "labour draft" (which in fact never came to much).

23 December 1944. "AMG" denoted "Allied Military Government", instituted in Germany, Italy, Austria and Japan. The idea of dismembering Germany after the war into up to six separate states was current in Allied plans at the time.

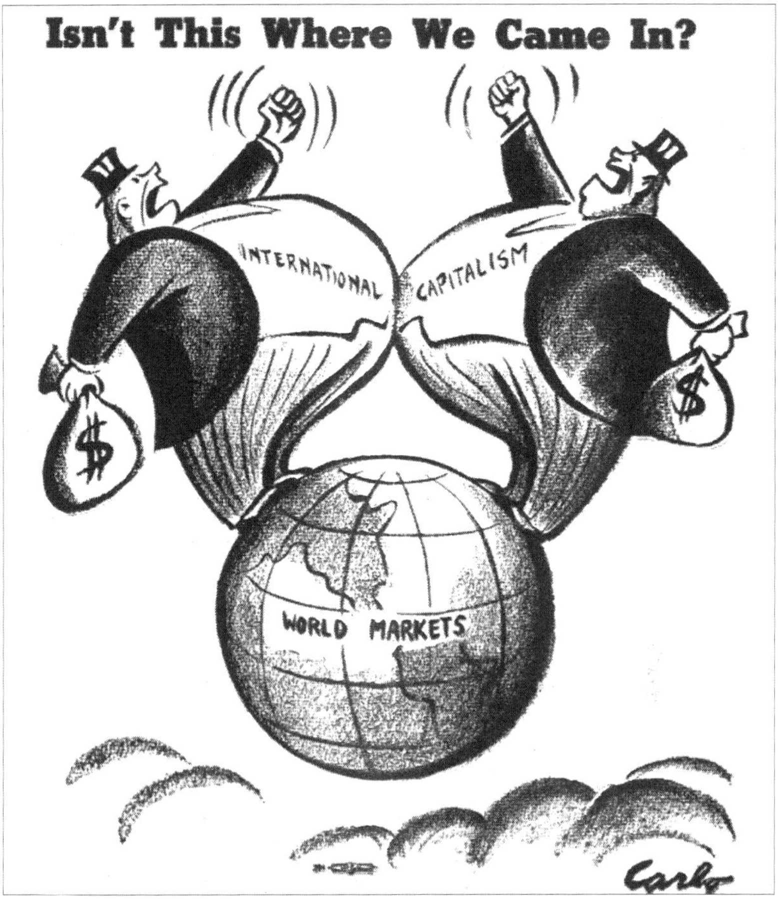

Above: 26 June 1944. Right: 31 March 1945. The smaller figure is inscribed "Small Nations". The words here are typical of 1930s gangster movies.

27 August 1945

10 September 1945

Above: 28 July 1945. Right: 18 August 1945.

11 February 1946

17 September 1945.

5 November 1945

Conquered Germany

2 April 1945. The defeat of Germany in May 1945 was followed by partition and economic devastation, sharpened by an influx of at least 12 million Germans expelled from or fleeing East Prussia, Poland, and elsewhere in Eastern Europe. Even in the US and British sectors of occupied Germany, during the very cold winter of 1946–47, Germans got from 1,000 to 1,500 calories per day, and mostly lacked fuel for heating. The USSR seized masses of industrial equipment from East Germany and moved it to the USSR, and used millions of German prisoners of war as slave labour.

Dividing Up the Booty

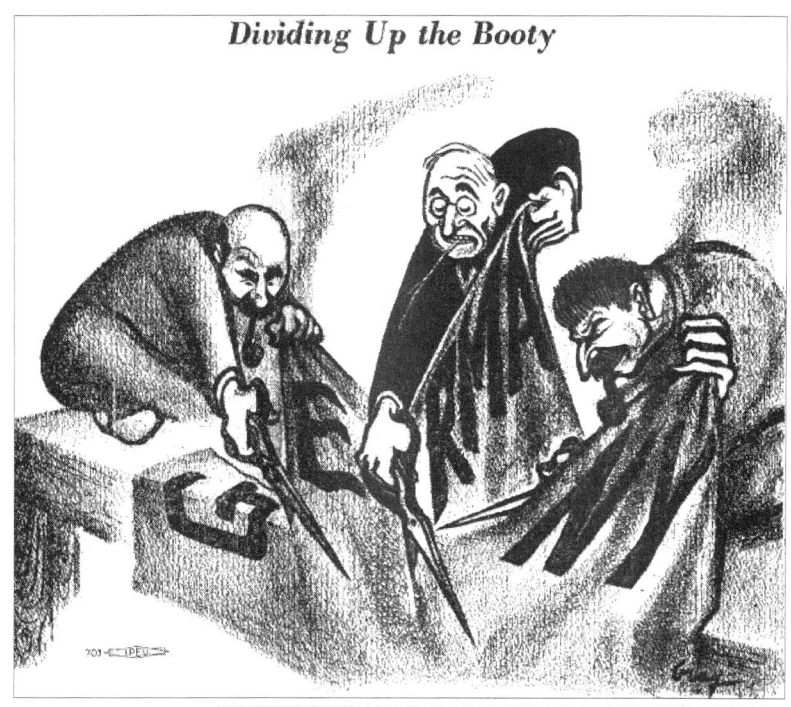

Above: 11 August 1945. The figures are Attlee, Truman, and Stalin, who divided Germany into their respective "occupation zones" (plus another for France). Right: 23 April 1945.

17 March 1945. The Yalta conference of Stalin, Churchill, and Roosevelt to do deals about the post-war world was in February 1945. The figure in the lower panel is Stalin.

Above: 17 April 1950. Trotskyists were jailed in Stalinist East Germany as they had been in Nazi Germany. Below: 17 March 1945.

The hope of humanity: a working-class socialist revolution

26 April 1943

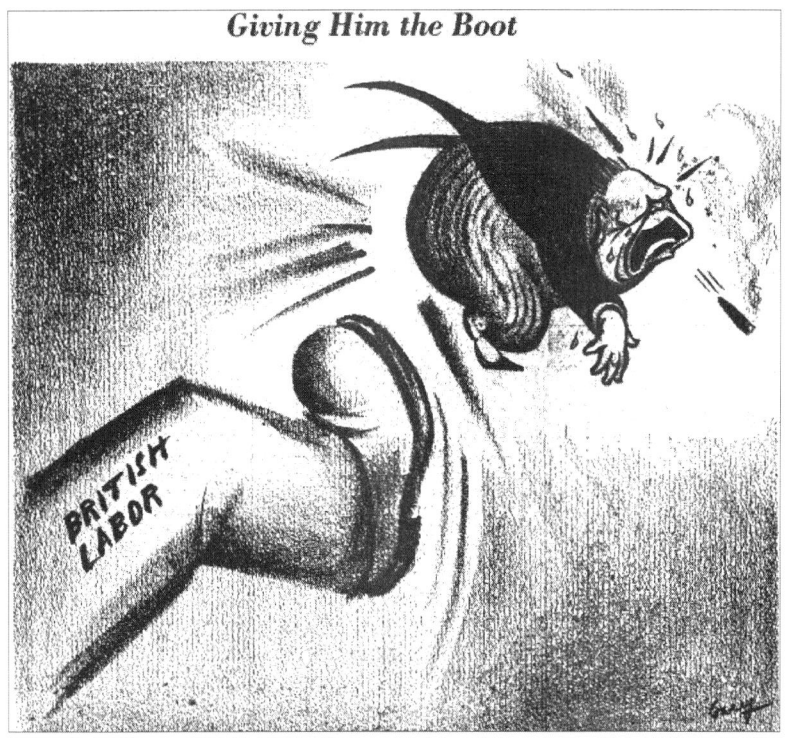

Above: 4 August 1945, after the British Labour Party's general election victory in July 1945 against Winston Churchill and the Tories. Below: 23 September 1944. The figures are US union leaders.

Unfurling the Trotskyist Banner

Left: 30 September 1944. The collapse of Mussolini's regime in Italy, in July 1943, and his successors' switch to the Allied side in the war, in September 1943, was followed by a workers' radicalisation, and armed uprising in the North, as well as heavy fighting between Allied and German forces in Italy. Below: 20 February 1943.

There was a tremendous upsurge of working-class militancy at the end of the war, but the Stalinist parties had the leadership of the working class and there was no working-class victory. The Stalinist entered coalition governments in France and Italy (until 1947) and help repress and control the working class. In Greece, Belgium, France, Italy, Indochina, Trotskyists were murdered by the Stalinists. They remained tiny organisations, and declined spectacularly from 1948.

They're All Afraid of It

Extend the October Revolution!

2 November 1935

30 April 1938

Above: 25 August 1945. *La Vérité* was the main French Trotskyist paper: the "Free French" government kept it illegal as under Nazi occupation for two years. De Gaulle's renegade-socialist minister André Malraux was directly responsible. Right: 29 April 1946.

10 October 1938

22 June 1942. From 1942 to 1944 the Stalinists and others campaigned for the US and UK to open a "second front" by invading Nazi-held continental Europe and thus relieve the pressure of German forces on the USSR. The "Third Front" meant working-class struggle politically independent from the existing blocs — in World War 2, in the Cold War, and in all circumstances.

Above:
9 Sep 1944.
Right:
19 Jan 1946

15 October 1945

The Only Road

Above: 4 November 1944. Right: September 1925.

12
In the shadow of nuclear war

"The attempt of the bourgeoisie during its internecine conflict to oblige humanity to divide up into only two camps is motivated by a desire to prohibit the proletariat from having its own independent ideas. [This must] give way to a third, independent, sovereign camp of the proletariat, that camp upon which, in point of fact, the future of humanity depends".
— Leon Trotsky

"Let's Negotiate, Gentlemen"

13 October 1945. The London Conference of Foreign Ministers was held in September 1945, and was inconclusive. The development by the US a of an atomic bomb changed world politics. When Russia developed a nuclear bomb in 1949, that created a world dominated by fear of the annihilation of civilisation if not of humankind itself. This balance of terror would in fact rule out full-scale war between the USA and Russia. There were a number of proxy wars between the great powers, most importantly in Korea. Right: 26 April 1947. Previous page: 9 September 1944.

The atomic bomb

Above: 26 April 1954. Below: 31 December 1945.

31 August 1946

10 September 1945. In the mid-50s this cartoon was cited by the US government to prove "subversiveness" when the "heterodox" Trotskyists of the Independent Socialist League went to court to get removed from the official list of "subversive organisations".

Wall Street And The Wonderful Lamp

20 April 1946

A bipolar world

6 October 1947

Above: 18 March 1946. The figures are Stalin, British prime minister Attlee, and US president Truman. Right: 4 November 1946

Above: 15 May 1950. Right: 23 February 1948

271

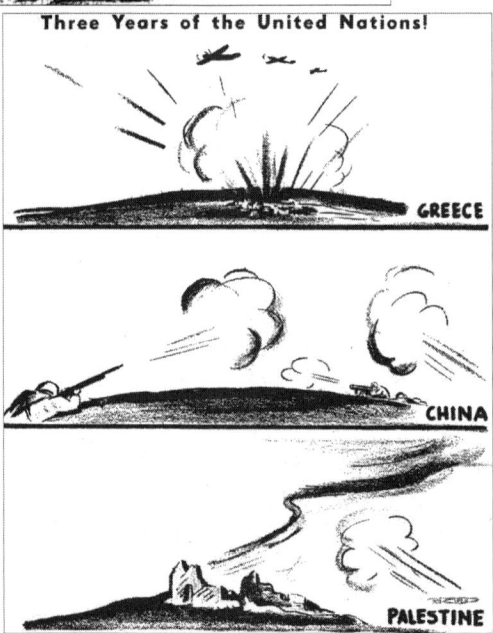

Above: 3 February 1947. The cooks are US president Truman, British prime minister Attlee, and Stalin. Right: 31 May 1948

"Liberated" Europe!

Above: 1 March 1948. Right: 26 August 1946. James F Byrnes was US Secretary of State, 1945-7: Vyacheslav Molotov was the USSR's foreign minister

Stalin's Empire

The Camp Followers

12 April 1948

29 March 1948, after the coup which consolidated full Stalinist power in Czechoslovakia. Klement Gottwald was the leader of the Stalinists in Czechoslovakia. From the end of 1942 the Stalinist Russian armies advanced steadily until they had conquered half of Germany. The Stalinists gained control in Czechoslovakia, Poland, Romania, Bulgaria, Albania, East Germany, Yugoslavia, and, until the mid-1950s, Austria. By 1948 they had installed full-scale Stalinist regimes in most countries. In Yugoslavia the Tito Stalinists had led an autonomous movement to power without the help of the Russian army. They would break with Stalin's Russia in 1948.

Top: 13 July 1953, after the workers' rising of that month against Stalinism in East Germany. Adenauer was Chancellor of West Germany; Malenkov was then on top in the USSR after the death of Stalin. Right: 14 June 1948, commenting on fake election results in Czechoslovakia after the Stalinists took full power in February 1948. The USSR called its satellites in Eastern Europe "People's Democracies" or "New Democracies".

Above: 26 Nov 1956, when Hungarian workers rose against Stalinism and set up workers' councils. Below: 23 July 1956. Workers in Poznan, in Poland, had risen up against the Stalinist regime and for a while created workers' councils. Rebuking them is USSR leader Khrushchev, backed up by the ghost of Stalin.

The witch-hunt republic

23 February 1953. Julius and Ethel Rosenberg were sentenced to death in April 1951 on charges of spying for the USSR, and killed by electrocution in June 1953

Security – For Whom?

Burnt Offering

Above: 22 October 1951.
Right: 29 June 1953

Above: 4 April 1949. Below: 13 June 1949. In 1949 Ohio passed a law requiring unemployment compensation payments to take a loyalty oath.

Top: 26 Dec 1949. Below: 8 Jun 1953, days before Julius and Ethel Rosenberg were killed by the US government on charges of spying for the USSR.

Above: 31 May 1948. The Mundt Bill authorised international operations like Voice of America, but also banned their broadcast within the USA (because the State Department was considered leftish). Right: 7 December 1953. The speaker is McCarthy; looking on are Hitler and Mussolini.

Liberty Put to the Stake

6 July 1953. Senator Joseph McCarthy compiled a list of 30,000 books to be removed from 258 overseas libraries of the US Information Service, and many books were removed or burned. They included thrillers like *The Maltese Falcon* and *The Thin Man*. Two medical books were purged because they "unduly stressed Negro medical statistics". Gunnar Myrdal's *An American Dilemma* (on racial discrimination in the USA) was banned. So, oddly, was Whittaker Chambers' *Witness*, a diatribe against the Communist Party written after he left it. The figures setting the books on fire are inscribed "State Dep't" and "McCarthy".

22 September 1952. In the 1930s and during the war the American Communist Party built up a tremendous network of front organisations. It has control of a number of trade unions. It was very popular during the war, when the Russians were very popular. It played a full part in witch hunting "Trotsky-fascists". It ardently supported the jailing of 18 leaders of the Socialist Workers Party and declared full support for "free enterprise". It was a dedicated strike-breaker and scab-herder in every real or threatening industrial dispute. As the Cold War developed the Stalinist party was winkled out of its positions of power. Its influence was questioned everywhere, its members declared foreign agents, spies, conspirators. The government started a purge of CPers in the civil service in 1947. The purge spread as Cold War hysteria gripped the country, and all socialists were targeted. After 1950 the hysteria took on the name of Senator Joe McCarthy.

US imperialism

23 April 1938. Roosevelt announced a "Good Neighbour Policy", chiefly towards Latin America, in 1933. The US came out of the war as the greatest power on the planet. It buttressed reactionary regimes which it thought would block Stalinism. It took responsibility for shoring up the old great imperialist powers, while simultaneously exerting a pressure on them to liquidate the old colonial empires. The USA itself did not need old-style colonies. World affairs came to be polarised between the two great powers, the USA and Russia.

Above: 13 October 1941. W F Knox had become Secretary of the Navy in 1940. Right: 26 May 1947. The flag showing the recipient of the $400 million loan is inscribed "Greek reaction"

2 May 1939. The bayoneted figure is inscribed: "Latin American people"

Above: 10 March 1945. The emaciated arms are inscribed "Greece", "Belgium", "France", "Italy". Below: 31 May 1947

"It's Your Turn Now"

Above: 30 March 1946. The paper in the cop's hand reads "Draft Extension" (conscription was continued after the war); the gravestone is inscribed "Killed In Action". Right: 5 April 1947. The Truman Doctrine, announced in March 1947 by US President Harry Truman (pictured), was that the US would intervene with aid and militarily to stop the spread of Stalinism.

9 August 1948. Douglas MacArthur, effective ruler of Japan under US military occupation, cracked down on strikes in 1948. 22 March 1947. "The helping hand" was a catchphrase of US President Truman, but the US was aiding right-wingers in Greece in civil war, also supported by the British, against Stalinist-led forces.

Above: "By this sign we conquer". Below: "The Diploma". The Kellogg Pact, an agreement supposedly to renounce war, named after US Secretary of State Kellogg, was signed was signed by Germany, France and the United States on 27 August 1928

A permanent arms economy

9 February 1948. The fuse on the "war" barrel is the US Air Policy Commission, which on 1 Jan 1948 had urged a big expansion of the US airforce. On the "depression" barrel it is the Economic Report to Congress. US military spending, after dipping briefly after 1945, rose at the end of the 1940s and even faster during the Korean war of 1950-3. It remained high from then to today, and the great slew of industrial contracts thus created was widely reckoned to be a big factor in keeping capitalism buoyant.

Above: 31 July 1950. Below: 2 February 1953. Charles Wilson, boss of General Motors, told Senate confirmation hearings for his appointment as Secretary of Defense that year: "What's good for General Motors is good for the country".

Above: 9 May 1955. Below: 20 October 1939. "The forgotten man" was a famous Roosevelt catchphrase from a 1932 speech.

13
World War 3?

"Some victorious state may, as a result of the war, unify the entire world in a totalitarian vice. But even if such a hypothesis should be realised, which is highly doubtful, military 'unification' would have no greater stability than the Versailles treaty. National uprisings and pacifications would culminate in a new world war, which would be the grave of civilisation. Not our subjective wishes but the objective reality speaks for it, that the only way out for humanity is the world socialist revolution" — Leon Trotsky, The USSR in War

Colonial revolts

The Wounded Killer

"What characterizes Bolshevism on the national question is that in its attitude toward oppressed nations, even the most backward, it considers them not only the object but also the subject of politics... Bolshevism penetrates into the midst of the oppressed nations; it raises them up against their oppressors; it ties up their struggle with the struggle of the proletariat in capitalist countries; it instructs the oppressed Chinese, Hindus, or Arabs in the art of insurrection and it assumes full responsibility for this work in the face of civilized executioners" — Leon Trotsky, What Next?

Above: 6 Oct 1944. The small figures threatening insurgent Indochina are inscribed "Attlee", "De Gaulle", "Hirohito" (emperor of Japan), and "Truman". Page 297: 28 January 1952. The figures are Truman, French military chief Juin, and Churchill. Right: 25 July 1927. The radical movement led by Sandino in Nicaragua was fighting US forces and local conservatives. Page 298: 23 August 1948.

27 June 1925

Above: 4 March 1946. As the colonial peoples pull, the chain of British imperialism is breaking in India, Palestine, Egypt, and Indonesia (where British troops were fighting the movement for independence from the Netherlands). Right: 19 October 1942. Stalinists were calling for the US and UK to invade continental Europe to create a "Second Front" and relieve pressure on US forces.

2 March 1942. Britain repressed mobilisations for independence in India in 1942.

Above: 24 August 1942. An emergency "whipping law" of the British colonial administration in India, of 1941, called for "rioters" to be punished by flogging.

Above: 19 November 1945. The Netherlands recognised the independence of Java and the rest of Indonesia in late 1949, after four years' fighting. The vulture is inscribed "Atlantic Charter" (the charter for NATO). Right: 18 August 1947

Korea

18 December 1950. The figure is US president Truman

Above: 25 Dec 1950. Below: 30 April 1951. Douglas MacArthur was US commander in Korea

Above: 8 January 1951. Below: 19 March 1951

Towards a Third World War?

5 April 1948. The figures represent US President Truman and USSR dictator Stalin

State of the Union, 1949

10 January 1949

Above: 23 February 1948. Right: 24 June 1946

MOVE OVER, BUDDY, DEMOCRACY IS BEING SAVED AGAIN!

"Dove of Peace"

Above: 19 April 1948. Right: 11 April 1949. NATO (the Atlantic Pact) was set up in 1949.

Above: 12 July 1948. Right: 26 April 1948.

For International Solidarity!

The Real Agenda!

Above: 24 April 1950. Right: 2 September 1946.

27 August 1951

Their Bid to German Militarism

Above: 7 April 1952. From the early 1950s both German states, disarmed after 1945, were rearmed. The figures are US president Truman and USSR leader Stalin. Right: 19 January 1953. Dwight D Eisenhower, a former US army general, became president in 1953.

The Inaugural Ball

30 April 1945